Praise for *Going Global*

"This is a book that any manager in today's fast changing global environment will find not just an enjoyable read, but an instructive one. There are insights and lessons on every page."
> —Christopher Bartlett, professor, Harvard Business School, author of *Transnational Management* and *Managing the Global Firm*

"The interviewees in *Going Global* are the men and women in the trenches of today's new, worldwide integrated economy. Webber and Taylor accurately capture the feelings and experiences of those facing the volley of change head-on and emerging victorious."
> —George Stalk, Jr., senior vice-president, The Boston Consulting Group, author of *Competing Against Time*

"Business leaders interested in the changing world economy will find plenty of useful tips here."
> —*Publishers Weekly*

"Webber and Taylor, early champions of the new economy, bring you a powerful look at what it will take to be successful in the global marketplace. A must read!"
> —Regis McKenna, chairman, Gemini/McKenna High Tech Strategies, author of *The Regis Touch* and *Who's Afraid of Big Blue*

"Bill Taylor and Alan Webber have captured the spirit of the brave new times in *Going Global*. Nice job!"
> —Tom Peters, coauthor of *In Search of Excellence* and author of *Thriving on Chaos* and *The Pursuit of Wow!*

PENGUIN BOOKS

GOING GLOBAL

William C. Taylor and Alan M. Webber are the founding editors of *Fast Company*, a magazine of ideas and tools for the new world of business. Previously, they were editors at the *Harvard Business Review*. Taylor is coauthor of *No-Excuses Management* and *The Big Boys: Power and Position in American Business*. Webber is coauthor of *Changing Alliances: The Harvard Business School Project on the Future of the Automobile Industry*. They live in Boston.

GOING GLOBAL

FOUR ENTREPRENEURS MAP THE NEW WORLD MARKETPLACE

William C. Taylor
Alan M. Webber

PENGUIN BOOKS

PENGUIN BOOKS
Published by the Penguin Group
Penguin Books USA Inc., 375 Hudson Street,
New York, New York 10014, U.S.A.
Penguin Books Ltd, 27 Wrights Lane, London W8 5TZ, England
Penguin Books Australia Ltd, Ringwood, Victoria, Australia
Penguin Books Canada Ltd, 10 Alcorn Avenue,
Toronto, Ontario, Canada M4V 3B2
Penguin Books (N.Z.) Ltd, 182–190 Wairau Road,
Auckland 10, New Zealand

Penguin Books Ltd, Registered Offices:
Harmondsworth, Middlesex, England

First published in the United States of America by Viking Penguin,
a division of Penguin Books USA Inc. 1996
Published in Penguin Books 1997

1   3   5   7   9   10   8   6   4   2

Published by arrangement with Whittle Communications L.P.

THE LIBRARY OF CONGRESS HAS CATALOGUED THE HARDCOVER AS FOLLOWS:
Taylor, William C.
Going global: four entrepreneurs map the new world marketplace/
William C. Taylor, Alan M. Webber.
p.   cm.
ISBN 0-670-86308-4 (hc.)
ISBN 0 14 02.4899 4 (pbk.)
1. International business enterprises.   2. Entrepreneurship.
3. International finance.   I. Webber, Alan M., date.   II. Title.
HD2755.5.T435   1996
338.8′8—dc20   95–21255

Printed in the United States of America
Set in Sabon

CONTENTS

TERRA INCOGNITA

The most promising words ever written on the maps of human knowledge are terra incognita— *unknown territory.*

—DANIEL J. BOORSTIN, *THE DISCOVERERS*

The drive to explore marks the great advances in every age of human history. In the late fifteenth century, as Librarian of Congress Emeritus Daniel J. Boorstin relates in his celebrated book *The Discoverers,* the convergence of knowledge, technology, financial resources, and hands-on skill combined to open up a New World—a world of vast riches and opportunity, uncertainty and suffering, and constant change.

Today we are witnessing a similar burst of exploration: businessmen and -women are opening up a New Economy, a global economy marked by speed, innovation, and knowledge. A powerful set of economic and technological imperatives is reshaping not only the rules and practice of business, but also its logic. Today the status quo is a prescription for disaster. Companies know that they must learn; they must adapt rapidly and dramatically to unexpected challenges and demands; they must innovate in products and in processes; they must create new value for their customers and give new latitude to their employees.

These imperatives are producing a new business dynamic around the world. Today we live and work in a global economy in which companies routinely cross established national boundaries to compete for markets and customers; an economy in which companies take themselves apart and put themselves back together in new configurations, creating new alliances and relationships, including attacks on former partners and partnerships with former competitors; an economy built on knowledge, innovation, speed, and quality; an economy in which change—fast-paced, relentless, and dispassionate—is the order of the day.

The New Economy raises strategic questions: In a global economy, where do I look for my next competitor? Who are my potential allies? It raises organizational questions: In a global company, how do I combine the power of worldwide scale with the speed and responsiveness necessary to succeed in local markets? It raises product questions: In a global marketplace, must my company offer the same products and services all around the world? In short, what are the new ideas and practices that will fit the new global economy?

Today, just as in the earlier Age of Discovery, a few global explorers are out ahead of the curve of change. They are the business innovators who are not merely identifying the changes or speculating on what should be done, but are out making the decisions that drive and guide the new world economic order. And like the earlier generation of global explorers, these business explorers fill four distinct roles; merging the languages of business and exploration, they are the Captain, the Mapmaker, the First Mate, and the Financier. Together they represent a template for change and embody the know-how that companies must have today to compete in the global economy.

As in any voyage, first there is the Captain, the leader with the vision and drive to carry the exploration forward. The Captain we have chosen is David Whitwam, chairman and CEO of Whirlpool Corporation, the world's largest manufacturer of home appliances. The apparently stable and traditional world of dishwashers, refrigerators, and washing machines may seem an unlikely place to find a global pioneer. But since 1987, when Whitwam became CEO, Whirlpool has been a company with a mission. Over the last eight years, it has assembled a global web of factories, R&D centers, and powerful brands—KitchenAid, Roper, Estate, Admiral, Ignis, Laden, Bauknecht, and, of course, Whirlpool. As a result, Whirlpool is now the only global player in its industry and a strategic innovator that is driving change and forcing its rivals to struggle to keep pace.

In effecting this transformation, Whitwam has grappled with the issues facing all CEOs in the New Economy. He has reinvented Whirlpool's strategy based on the realities of global competition, redesigned the company's organizational structure to fit that strategy, and identified the new skills his managers and workers must master if the global organization is to perform and deliver.

Whitwam's insights and experiences offer valuable guidance to business leaders who are about to embark on a similar voyage. He makes it clear that the central requirement is a collection of people prepared to make a potentially hazardous journey. As he says, "Only one aspect of this whole globalization process still keeps me up at night: Do we have the skills to pull it off? The strategy is right. What worries me is, can we implement the strategy?"

The second critical role in any exploration is that of the Mapmaker, the person who pieces together reports from previous voyages to draw the charts the Captain relies upon. It is the Mapmaker's open mind and questioning spirit that make it possible to redraw the commonly accepted map of the world and suggest an alternative way of arranging things. As Boorstin writes about the mapmakers of old, "The openings in the mind preceded and made possible the struggles for the openings on the sea."

To exemplify the mind of the Mapmaker, we have chosen Kenichi Ohmae, former chairman of McKinsey & Company's Tokyo office. He is one of the world's leading business consultants and an authority on globalization. In the early 1980s, Ohmae was among the first business thinkers to recognize the emergence of a commercially borderless world. Since then he has been a prominent and unwavering voice, writing, lecturing, and consulting on the changing shape of the world map. In his 1987 book, *Beyond National Borders*, he concluded that traditional boundaries "are virtually meaningless today. In our new economic system, cooperation and interdependence, not conflict and independence, are prerequisites for survival."

Ohmae's thinking has guided CEOs and top executives around the world who are dealing with the strategic issues raised by the New Economy. The map that Ohmae draws is vastly different from the traditional maps found in an airline guide or a world atlas. He sees a world organized on two levels: an overarching triad of giant countries in Asia, Europe, and North America supplemented by emerging regions and subregions that defy national boundaries. In fact, Ohmae believes that our most familiar unit of analysis—the nation-state—is obsolete and unhelpful. "The outmoded unit of 'the nation' makes it much harder for business leaders to make sound, informed choices about their strategies and organizations," he says. "Nation-states have become unnatural, even dysfunctional."

Last year, Ohmae left McKinsey & Company to take up the cause of political reform in Japan. While he continues to write and consult on matters of business strategy as managing director of the Yokohama Consulting Group, Ohmae's new commitment is to implement his vision about the future of the global economy in the political arena. Indeed, he went so far as to run for the office of governor of Tokyo.

On every successful voyage of discovery there is also a strong, capable, trustworthy First Mate, the member of the crew to whom the Captain looks for day-to-day, hands-on management, the person who works most closely with the others on the ship to make sure everyone pulls together. The First Mate we have selected is Barbara Kux, vice-president of Switzerland's Nestlé, the world's largest food company, and a former president of ABB Power Ventures, a subsidiary of the Swedish-Swiss manufacturing giant Asea Brown Boveri.

For the past six years, Kux has dedicated herself to the difficult work of bringing change to Eastern Europe. She has taught managers there the basics of competition, built profitable companies in a region racked with political turmoil, and wrestled successfully with the challenges of poor quality and massive inefficiency. In the process, she has developed practical approaches to creating change across borders—approaches that work and that should be instructive to managers seeking to inculcate world-class performance in global operations.

"The single most important reality of working in the global economy is constant change," Kux says. "The only way managers can prepare themselves for such rapid-fire change is to constantly introduce change into their own lives—to seek out different environments, different functions, different companies, different industries."

The last critical role in any exploration belongs

to the Financier. Throughout history, the Financier has played a vital, if hidden, role. In fact, in the earlier Age of Discovery, the Financier was not only responsible for funding the journey; often it was his canny judgment that determined whether or not a history-shaping voyage would be made in the first place. Queen Isabella gets credit for supporting Columbus's voyage to the New World, but it was her financial adviser who persuaded the wavering monarch that the investment was sound. In the New Economy, the Financier plays a similar role, offering advice, experience, contacts around the world—and, perhaps least important, access to capital.

Our Financier is John Doerr, a partner at Kleiner Perkins Caufield & Byers and one of the country's most influential, creative, and unconventional venture capitalists. Doerr and his partners in the San Francisco–based firm have funded a remarkable collection of technology companies: Lotus Development Corporation, Sun Microsystems Corporation, Cypress Semiconductor Corporation, Compaq Computer Corporation, Genentech Inc., to name a few. (Doerr has also become an investor in, and adviser to, the authors' new publishing company.) In the process Doerr has contributed his expertise, knowledge, and experience to the emergence of the web of companies that comprise the industries of "bits and bytes, bugs and drugs," helping create $100 billion of economic value in the span of a decade—"the single largest creation of new wealth in the history of the planet," as he likes to say.

But beyond the notable achievement of creating vast wealth is an even greater achievement: creating a global web of relationships that makes it possible for business leaders to connect with one another all over the world, and formulating a clear vision of what really matters in the world of business. Because of his distinctive approach to venture capital, much of what Doerr says runs counter to conventional wisdom. He rejects the romantic image of "cowboy capitalists," for example. Instead he sees a world of relationships and joint ventures, of savvy businesspeople crossing boundaries to combine Japan's manufacturing skills with Silicon Valley's software know-how. Doerr even goes against the grain when it comes to defining the larger purpose of his work. If the choice is between making a difference and making a profit, he says, "I'd vote for making a difference."

The four individuals you will meet in this book come from different backgrounds, different nations, and different industries, and have had vastly different personal experiences. What they share, however, is a passion for exploration. Like all great discoverers, they set out not to find what is unknown, but to demonstrate that what they know to be true about the world is, in fact, true. They hold strong convictions about business and competition, strategy and organization. They go beyond pithy slogans and easy talk to live their ideas through crisp, bold, and uncompromising action.

After having read these interviews, you will undoubtedly come away with your own lessons and insights. There is certainly no one right way to become a global company, no single approach to strategy, finance, or organization that will apply to every company and every business situation. But reading across the stories of these four exceptional innovators, we find a number of compelling themes that may point the way for future global explorers:

1. In the New Economy, companies compete on the basis of knowledge. At the beginning of the industrial era, "factor endowments" such as natural resources or a favorable location played a critical role in determining competitive success. As the industrial economy matured, scale and scope became powerful forces. In the New Economy, power comes from knowledge. It can be a new business model advanced by an entrepreneur, a competitive insight contributed by a strategist, a better technique on the manufacturing line devised by an hourly worker. Whatever form they take, knowledge, ideas, and creativity are the essential attributes of winning organizations.

2. Great companies implement relentlessly. Ideas may be the coin of the realm, but implementation remains the test of any successful company. The reason is simple: In a global economy, where speed and nimbleness are vital attributes, ideas stay proprietary for only a moment. They offer companies a head start, not a permanent advantage. What matters is execution, followed by another round of innovation and creativity, followed by a renewed commitment to execution.

3. The essential factor in business is people. That may seem counterintuitive; after all, the New Economy is propelled by faster and faster technology, instant communications, borderless companies, and fluid capital. Yet people matter more than ever—and more than any other element. Put simply, the quality of a company cannot exceed the quality of the people who choose to work there.

4. Leaders need a new kind of vision—a parallax view. Vision is not about lofty mission statements or philosophical pronouncements. Vision, ultimately, is about seeing. In particular, vision in the New Economy is about seeing two fields at the same time: being able to scan the whole world, identifying the important commonalities that unify nations, markets, consumers, and suppliers, and being able to identify small pockets of communities around the world with distinctive tastes, wants, needs, and customs. The challenge is not to "think globally, act locally." It is to think globally, think locally, and act on both levels simultaneously.

5. Innovators in the New Economy want to have "serious fun." Business today is not just about hard work, it's also about a spirit of adventure. Change is challenging: The work is demanding, the stakes are high, the pressure is intense, the hours are long. But the opportunity to be part of a moment of epochal discovery and history-making invention is also exhilarating.

Indeed, the unforgiving demands of the times are matched only by the rewards of the undertaking: a chance to test yourself against the best, to stretch your thinking and experiences, to engage in enterprises and ventures never before possible. It is the kind of spirit that makes for memorable voyages, remarkable adventures, classic wrecks, and, as always, dramatic discoveries.

We hope the telling of these stories will provide the opportunity for others to learn from them—and to go beyond them.

GOING
GLOBAL

THE CAPTAIN

DAVID WHITWAM

Chairman and CEO,
Whirlpool Corporation

Few people would associate the world of home appliances—dishwashers, ranges, refrigerators, microwave ovens—with global innovation and strategic change. But David Whitwam, chairman and CEO of Whirlpool Corporation, is every bit as daring and driven as his colleagues in more glamorous industries. In many respects his achievements are even more remarkable.

Whirlpool came of age in simpler times. For most of its history, since it sold its first washing machine in 1911, the company made appliances for one market (the United States) and sold most of them through one customer (Sears, Roebuck & Company). Its factories, based in small towns in

Michigan, South Carolina, Arkansas, and else-where, did things more or less the same way year after year. They built the same products, used the same technologies, bought parts from the same suppliers. Whirlpool was satisfied. And why not? It was a leading company in the largest appliance market in the world.

Fast-forward to the era of David Whitwam. To-day, in an intensely competitive global economy, the world seems less secure. Being number one at home doesn't count for what it used to; it's more like being a big fish in a medium-sized pond. Eu-rope is nearly as large a market for appliances as the United States. The market in Asia is growing four times as fast as the market in America—and will soon be larger than that of the United States.

Meanwhile, doing things the same way has be-come a prescription for disaster disguised as stabil-ity. Technology moves faster than ever, even in appliances, and high-quality components can come from anywhere. A compressor, the key technology inside a refrigerator, is just as likely to come from Brazil, Italy, or Japan as from Kentucky or Indi-ana. Whirlpool's engineers are competing with en-gineers from all over the world, not just with their U.S. counterparts at General Electric or Maytag.

David Whitwam's tenure at Whirlpool has been dedicated to addressing these and other global challenges—and addressing them more decisively than any other CEO in his industry, or most other industries for that matter. Whitwam became CEO in 1987. Since then he has driven the company to-ward a single, compelling goal: to become a more formidable competitor in every market it serves by being the only global competitor in the market. Through a series of acquisitions, strategic alliances, and joint ventures, it has assembled a global web of factories, brands, and R&D centers. Its most daring move came in 1991, when it acquired the appliance business of Philips, the troubled Dutch manufacturing conglomerate. (The billion-dollar deal got its start in 1989, when Whirlpool and Philips created a joint venture to sell appliances. Two years later Whirlpool became the venture's sole owner.) With the stroke of a pen, Whirlpool became the third-largest appliance company in Europe, taking the biggest risk in its eighty-year history. All told, Whirlpool builds appliances in eleven countries and sells them under ten major brand names.

The results speak for themselves. Whirlpool is the only global player in its industry, a strategic innovator whose rivals are struggling to keep pace. It generates annual revenues of roughly $8 billion (more than double the level of the mid-1980s) and employs nearly forty thousand people. More important, it is creating value. In 1990 the company's shares traded at under $25, and its total stock-market value was $1.6 billion. Five years later Whirlpool shares were trading as high as $70, and its total market value was more than $5 billion.

The story of Whirlpool under David Whitwam is a story about strategy, technology, and competitiveness. But most of all, it is a story about change in the new global economy: initiating it, implementing it, overcoming resistance to it. And as described by Whitwam in the conversation that follows, it is a story with lessons for companies in all kinds of industries. Plenty of CEOs speak the language of globalization. David Whitwam is in the throes of delivering on its promise. Much remains to be done, but he has the time to do it. At age fifty-four, Whitwam can be expected to remain at Whirlpool's helm throughout the decade.

These days it's hard to find a big-company CEO who's not trying to build a global organization. Why did you start down this road?

DAVID WHITWAM: We didn't wake up one morning and say, "We want to be a global company." In fact the appliance business today is not a global business in the strict sense of the word: We can't build identical products in a few factories and sell them around the world. A refrigerator is big and bulky and expensive to ship. So are many of the raw materials that go into it. With just a few exceptions, we have to build our products where we sell them.

On the other hand, all the market analyses we've done, all the best strategic thinking we've come up with, make it clear to us that appliances are becoming a global business. That means we have two options: We can wait for our competitors to make it happen and say, "We want to be like those companies." Or we can get out in front, shape the globalization of this industry, and let other people try to catch up with us. We're pursuing the second option.

What did you see to persuade you that appliances were becoming global? What's the strategic logic behind globalization?

We began to rethink our strategy in 1986. We were a very successful company. We had a dominant market share in the United States. We were creating decent returns for our shareholders. We were getting more efficient, which meant some head-count reductions, especially among managers, but we weren't in crisis like the auto industry or the steel industry. We made good products, offered solid jobs, provided stable career paths. Our people were satisfied.

But there were clouds on the horizon. Our success was in a mature industry dominated by a few big players: Whirlpool, General Electric, Maytag, Frigidaire. These four companies accounted for 90 percent of the 40 million appliances sold each year. We slugged it out on price and worked like hell to reduce costs: a few dollars out of the assembly process here, fewer defects and rework there. It was a low-margin industry, and it was a slow-growth industry—2 percent or 3 percent per year. We concluded that it was going to be very tough for Whirlpool to grow in this environment. And as a public company, we have to grow to create value.

We considered lots of strategic alternatives: acquisitions in the United States, financial restructuring, diversification. We also examined what was happening in the appliance industry worldwide. We studied Europe, Asia, Latin America. Who were the players? What were the market trends? Were there opportunities for us?

What did you find?

Several things became clear. The reason we defined appliances as a slow-growth industry was because we restricted our vision to the United States. This business is growing by 7 or 8 percent per year in Asia. It's growing even faster in some of the big developing countries like Mexico, India, and Brazil. There are huge market opportunities once you extend your vision beyond the United States.

Second, consumers around the world are becoming more alike rather than less alike. There are still big differences in how people use appliances and what features they prefer. Europeans are much more concerned about energy efficiency and water conservation than Americans. In Japan, where fewer women have entered the work force than in the United States, housewives prefer to be more "involved" with their laundry. So twin-tub washers, where you transfer clothes by hand from the wash side to the spin side, still account for half of all washers sold there. That's unthinkable in the United States—twin tubs are considered a Third World technology. But these differences are holdovers from the past, not signs of the future.

The overwhelming trend is toward global convergence in consumer tastes and product features.

That's also true for the core technologies inside our products. The market for the compressor, the key component in a refrigerator, is absolutely global. Our factories in Italy and Brazil ship compressors to Whirlpool assembly plants around the world. They also sell compressors to lots of other appliance companies, and we buy compressors from Matsushita and other Asian suppliers. Even when refrigerators look a little different on the outside, the underlying technology is still basic refrigeration technology, whether it's in Malaysia or Brazil or Hungary. The levels of performance and quality vary, but the core technologies are the same.

The closer we looked, the more we said to ourselves, "This is becoming a global industry. One of these days someone is going to figure that out and build lots of competitive advantage. That someone should be us."

You've been working on globalization since you became CEO. How different is Whirlpool today?

In the mid-1980s we were a one-dimensional company. Nearly all our sales came from the United States. In fact, 40 percent of our sales came from *one customer*—Sears, for which we build Kenmore appliances.

Today we build products in eleven countries. We are the largest appliance manufacturer in the world, and the only company with a strategic presence in the world's four major markets: North America, which is Canada, Mexico, and the United States; Latin America, which is South America, Central America, and the Caribbean; Europe, both east and west; and Asia, including Japan, China, Australia, and the fast-growing countries of East Asia. Our strategy is different in each region. But we have a strategy for each, and we manage each region as a cohesive unit rather than as a collection of countries.

Let me give you a better sense of the strategic diversity. We are the number-one appliance company in the United States. But we are only number three in Europe, where we have ten plants in four countries. We are working hard to leverage those manufacturing assets and build our brand position there—and not just in western Europe. Our most significant growth is coming from central Europe. We have a joint venture in the Slovak Republic, and we have subsidiaries in Poland and Hungary.

We are number one in Latin America. In fact, our largest market-share position in the world is in Latin America. We have a major joint venture in Brazil. Two factories in Joinville build refrigerators, freezers, and air conditioners and employ 4,800 people. A plant in São Paulo makes ranges and employs nearly 1,500 people. We have a majority-owned business in Argentina—it's a great business, our most profitable market in the world in terms of [percentage] return on sales. But Argentina doesn't build everything it sells. Whirlpool Argentina makes refrigerators and assembles washers from kits it imports from Europe. It also receives products from our plants in Brazil. Countries like Venezuela and Colombia import our products from Brazil, Argentina, and the United States.

We embarked on a learning strategy for Asia in the late 1980s. Whirlpool had virtually no presence there, just a distributor in Taiwan. Since 1988 we've established subsidiaries in Taiwan, Hong Kong, Singapore, and Malaysia. There's an important joint venture in India. Sure, we're still a small player, but we are already the largest Western appliance company there. You can see the beginnings of a real business.

The next step is to make hard investments in plant and equipment. Today, half of what we sell in Asia comes from our plants in Europe and North America. The other half comes from Japanese and Korean companies that build products for us. We are going to build four or five plants, including a plant in China, and we are going to leverage those assets across Asia.

Plenty of U.S. executives still complain about how hard it is to crack Asia. Has it been tougher than you expected?

We're making progress. Look at Hong Kong. In three years, we have gone from virtually nothing there to the number-one position in laundry equipment. We ship washers to Hong Kong from our plant in Amiens, France. They're a terrific product, but that's not why we're successful. Our local managers studied the market and devised a unique strategy for customer service. We deliver washing machines in Hong Kong at any time—night or day, weekday or weekend—wherever customers want them. And we have an army of technicians, a couple of hundred well-trained people, who guarantee service on those washers within twenty-four hours. In a place as crowded and frenetic as Hong Kong, that's a real service. It's been a great success. It's all about adding value rather than merely competing on price, which anyone can do.

That's a remarkable expansion in just five years. Are all the strategic pieces now in place?

Don't get carried away with the pieces on the board. It's easy to conquer geography—to buy companies outside your home base, to build factories in Asia or Latin America, to plant flags. We are not planting flags. We are building a global enterprise.

What's the difference?

The difference is leverage and integration. Unless we leverage our assets and integrate the organization on a global scale—unless we are stronger in Brazil because of what we do in Italy, unless we are smarter in Hong Kong because of what we've learned in Mexico, unless we can apply our core technologies all around the world—the strategy is not going to work. One plus one must equal three, or we fail. Let me give you another example from Asia. We have an embryonic business in India today, a joint venture with a local company called TVS. We have a factory in Pondicherry that builds fifty thousand washing machines a year under the TVS brand. We have a 20 percent market share. But we are committed to India for the long pull. In fact, we are about to increase our ownership percentage in the joint venture and introduce the Whirlpool brand name.

Why? There are 800 million people in India, and 100 million people in the middle class who can afford washers. All those people receive satellite television from Hong Kong. And the Whirlpool brand, as I've said, is now the number-one washer in Hong Kong. Every day tens of millions of Indians are bombarded with ads for a brand they can't buy yet. Soon they will be able to. That's leverage.

So the key to globalization is to understand how your strategic position in one country improves your position in another?

There's much more to this than strategy. Globalization requires huge cultural changes. For seventy-five years Whirlpool was a successful, conservative Midwestern company. Our headquarters city, Benton Harbor, Michigan, has a population of thirteen thousand. Our American factories are in small towns like Oxford, Mississippi, and Evansville, Indiana. Suddenly everything is different. People are getting passports for the first time, flying to places they've never been, dealing with new cultures, struggling with strange languages. This is radical change.

It's been tough helping people get ready for that change. When we announced the Philips acquisition, I traveled to every location in the company, talked with our people, explained why it was so important. Most opposed the move. They thought, "We're going to spend a billion dollars on a company that has been losing money for ten years? We're going to take resources we could use right here and ship them across the Atlantic because we think this is becoming a 'global' industry? What the hell does that mean?"

They were right to worry. If the Philips acquisition had failed, Whirlpool could not have survived. It was really that big a deal.

I remember sitting in our plant in Clyde, Ohio, which makes clothes dryers. There were five hundred people in the audience. I got excited: "You folks are going to have the opportunity to work not just in Clyde, but maybe in Cassinetta, Italy, or Neunkirchen, Germany! How many of you would like to think about that as part of your career?" A thousand eyes looked straight down at the floor. They were scared to death that if they made eye contact with me, I would think it meant they wanted to be transferred. Today—and this is a sign of how far we've come—lots of people are eager for those experiences. People say, "I want that kind of career. It's to my advantage to spend time working outside the United States."

Most companies in your industry have not followed your lead. They've stayed at home. Play devil's advocate and make the case for why this is not a global business.

First you would argue that customers are profoundly different around the world and will stay that way, which means you have to design unique products for individual markets and that there is no cross-border leverage. Then you would argue that there are limits on worldwide manufacturing. The nature of our products is that there isn't all that much economic value relative to their size, and the margins are so low that transportation costs can be the difference between making a profit and losing money. Finally, you would argue that it's possible to reach efficient scale in local markets, that appliances aren't like automobiles. You don't have to build millions of refrigerators to match the cost structure of the big guys.

Everything we've done shows that we don't agree with those arguments, but there are plenty of executives who do. My position is clear. You can make all the debating points you want, but the reality doesn't change: This business is becoming more and more alike all over the world.

Let's go to the other extreme. Is there a product that really captures the strategic potential of globalization?

Microwave ovens are a good example. They are small, they are the same size everywhere, they more or less look the same. You can build a microwave in one or two factories and then ship it economically wherever you want. Microwaves have never been a major product for Whirlpool. But now, as a result of our global presence, we have a chance to make a difference.

Let's start with the United States. Here microwave ovens are a commodity. They are a food defroster, a hot-dog cooker, a way to warm up leftovers. They didn't start out so limited. This industry spent lots of time in the early days with in-store demonstrations and other tools to teach people how to use microwaves for "real" cooking. We didn't make much headway. Then came the invasion of the low-cost manufacturers from Japan and Korea. They defeatured them, competed solely on price, totally commoditized microwaves.

Now go to Europe. There is a large commodity microwave business in Europe—low price, few features, turn it on to defrost the chicken. But for a variety of reasons, Europe also held on to its high-end microwave business, where consumers use the product for real cooking. When we moved into Europe, we decided not to chase the commodity segment. It's almost impossible to make money on commodity microwaves.

But we also decided to keep pushing the high-end technology. Our microwave expertise is concentrated in Norrköping, Sweden. The engineers in our lab and plant know more about microwave technology than anyone else in the world. About eighteen months ago they launched a radical new technology, which we call the Whirlpool VIP. It is a crisping microwave; you can bake pies or chocolate-chip cookies and they come out crisp and brown. It is now the number-one microwave in Europe. And our factory has become one of the most competitive microwave factories in the world.

We have new technology and a competitive factory, which means we are in a position to roll out the microwave globally. We introduced the VIP to the United States in 1993, and we can't keep it on the shelves. Sure, the markets are still very different. It will take lots of persuasion for U.S. consumers to rethink how they use their microwaves. But we have the technology to do it, we know how European consumers use their microwaves, so we have a chance to innovate here, to change the game.

So global integration means being able to transfer products from one market to another quickly, whether it's washing machines in India or microwaves in the United States?

It's more than products or even the technology inside products. Integration applies to every aspect of the business: market research, relationships with the retail trade, customer service. Even brand identity. We are absolutely committed to building the Whirlpool name into a powerful global brand. That's new in this business. But we think it will create huge advantages for us, and we are one of the few companies in a position to do it.

Electrolux, our biggest competitor in Europe, manages thirty different brands there. We don't see how you do that effectively. When we bought Philips, we made it clear that we intended to build the Whirlpool brand name, first as a dual brand with Philips, then purely on its own. It was a risky strategy. Philips was a top brand in Europe; Whirlpool had zero recognition. But given our commitment to global integration, the Whirlpool name simply had to work.

As part of that strategy, we launched a $100 million advertising campaign. We were amazed to learn that Philips, which sold appliances in fourteen different European countries, used ten different agencies to create its ads! We used one advertising campaign for the entire continent—different languages, but the same message and the same creative. Our managers in Europe were vehemently opposed. They insisted that the French are different from the Spanish, that the Italians are different from the Germans. It wasn't true. We did lots of research, storyboarded lots of different campaigns. The same campaign scored highest in every single country. That's what we rolled out.

We may have been the first company in any industry to have a totally pan-European television advertising campaign. Can we do that globally?

Yes, we can. It's going to take some time, but we plan to do it. Again, it's the power of leverage.

Let's keep pushing those two critical words: leverage and integration. It sounds like you're talking about more than products, even more than global economies of scale. You're talking about expertise, learning, sharing what you know.

The United States has the most competitive appliance market anywhere. In most parts of the business, our market is ten to fifteen years ahead of the rest of the world. The whole retail area is a good example. In the United States, the most important trend over the last ten years has been the rise of power retailers: Sears Brand Central, Lechmere Inc., Fretters Inc., Circuit City Stores Inc. Giant stores, moving huge volumes, offering low prices and a wide variety of brands. U.S. appliance manufacturers have learned how to navigate in that environment—not because we're smarter than the Europeans or the Japanese, but because we've had to.

Europe has just begun to move in the direction of power retailing. Last year we held a big conference in Cannes, France, that brought together Europe's top two hundred appliance retailers. They represented 60 percent of all the white goods sold there. It was an interactive event. We got them in a big theater. We put computer terminals at all the chairs. We asked questions—for example, how many of them had definite plans, so definite they've taken them to their boards of directors, to cross borders and establish retail outlets in other countries. The answer was 90 percent. When power retailers take hold in Europe, we will be ready for it. The skills we've developed here are directly transferable.

It works the other way, too. Europe is the world's center of expertise in styling and design. What we learn in our European design labs is going to influence how we design products in Benton Harbor. Europe also does a much better job with noise than we do. The kitchens are smaller, and customers are more demanding about acceptable noise levels. When we bring Whirlpool managers from Europe to live here, it's one of the first things they notice: How can you people stand all that racket? We'll be able to transfer that expertise into our products.

Why aren't the Japanese a bigger force in the U.S. appliance market?

There are several reasons. First, there are no obvious vulnerabilities among U.S. companies. We constantly hammer one another to drive down costs, drive up quality, provide great service. There was no obvious gap for the Japanese to come in and exploit. If they wanted to invest resources outside Japan, why slug it out with three or four giants in the United States who were getting the job done?

I compare us to the auto industry in Japan. The intensity of domestic competition among the Japanese auto companies trained them to come into the United States. And the Japanese auto buyer is the most demanding customer in the world. If you understand how to serve car buyers in Japan, you can serve car buyers anywhere. That goes for appliance buyers in the United States.

There are other reasons. One is the sheer growth of the Asian market. The Japanese have such incredible opportunities in Asia alone—more than they can fund—that there's not a strategic urgency to come to North America. Why put your money in the United States, where you have 2 percent annual growth and four companies dominating the market? Why not stay in Asia, a market growing at up to 8 percent per year, the second-largest market in the world, the largest market in the world by 1996?

There's one last reason. The Japanese absolutely do not see appliances as a global business. I know because I've talked to the top executives. They do not see a disadvantage to their position at home if they do not participate in the world market.

Why, then, should you take on the Japanese in Asia?

We simply must be in the fastest-growing appliance market in the world, which will soon be the largest appliance market in the world. How could we survive, or grow at the rates we expect to grow at, without a presence in Asia? The real question is, Could we crack the Asian market if we were not a global player? I don't think so. We wouldn't have the capital, the people, the technology, the marketing know-how, to make the kinds of investments we are going to make over the next five years.

It goes back to the issue of leverage. There is not one Japanese appliance company as big as Whirlpool. Most of the companies, in terms of their sales inside Japan, are about one-third our size. So every yen they spend to develop a new product is spread over a much smaller volume base than every dollar we spend. We are not going into Asia and reinventing every product we sell. We will feature our products to meet distinct market needs, but we will leverage our component and process technologies—whether it's compressors for refrigerators or motors for dishwashers.

If we execute right, our global presence will give us a huge advantage in cracking these new markets. But it all comes back to integration. It's easy to plant flags. If we just set up a subsidiary in Thailand, build a plant in the Philippines, buy a company in Malaysia, we're not going to succeed. If all we do is manage these businesses as stand-alone operations, we won't be any stronger than our local rivals. Strength comes from integration.

We've talked a lot about strategy. Let's talk about the human side of globalization. Is there such a thing as a global manager?

Only one aspect of this whole globalization process still keeps me up at night: Do we have the skills to pull it off? The strategy is right. What worries me is, can we implement the strategy?

I worry because the skills and talents this company needs today are radically different from what we needed five years ago. It goes for me as much as anyone. I have been at Whirlpool for twenty-five years. I spent my entire career developing knowledge and skills for the kind of company we were then, not the kind of company we are now. We need lots of new skills in this organization.

Like what?

The most important skill is the capacity not only to manage change, but to create it. Our managers must thrive in an environment of constant uncertainty. That's not normal for people in general, and it's not normal for Whirlpool people in particular. We've been successful for a long time. We've been successful in an industry that has not been very eager to innovate. The washing machines we were selling in 1980 weren't all that different from what we were selling in 1950. The way we did business in 1980 was basically the way we did business in 1970, which was basically the way we did business in 1960. We just didn't do things radically different from year to year. Now we do things differently every year, which is why we spend so much time reinforcing the message of forced change. We are going to force change as a strategy in this company. We are going to force our competitors to react to us, rather than us react to them. It takes a different kind of manager to do that.

The second skill is to be comfortable with teamwork and ambiguity. Most people still prefer predictable rules and clear responsibilities. They like managing within organization charts. Where's my box? Where do the lines from my box go? What are my accountabilities?

Those one-dimensional relationships just don't work anymore. Whirlpool is a vastly more complex organization than it was five years ago. For us to succeed, our people have to be able to manage outside the boxes. They have to work across functions, geographies, business units, brands. The real work today takes place at the boundaries. That demands a different way of managing.

How is your job different today from when you became CEO in 1987?

What I do today is dramatically different from what I did six or seven years ago. In the early part of this process, I—or I should say we, the top management team—spent a huge amount of time directly managing change. Communicating with the organization about what was new and challenging in the world. Convincing the organization how urgent the need for change really was. Looking back, and I've told this to my people here, I feel like we communicated twice as much as I ever dreamed possible and half as much as we probably should have.

I also spent a lot of time on the operating side of the business—really getting involved with the details of what was going on in various countries and in various product lines. After all, we had made major acquisitions of businesses that had not been performing. And we made a decision not to change the leadership of those businesses. So by definition, we had to change how that leadership worked. That took a lot of operating time and attention from me. I had to help to build the management systems and operating principles in our new operations around the world.

Today I spend most of my time on the softer side of things, our global integration activities. Our people know how to manage their businesses. My job is to help them work together as a global team.

How does that work in practice? Is being physically on site around the world important for you?

It's absolutely important. I'm out of the country at least one week per month, sometimes more, and it should probably be lots more. By the way, my travel is not simply me as CEO flying to Italy or Hong Kong. It's not just "Here comes the CEO to evaluate your operation." It's me playing a role with Whirlpool people from around the world—Europeans, Americans, Asians—in meetings and events specifically geared to global integration:

product reviews, technology reviews, strategy reviews. I use my role as CEO to bring these people together, push them to work together as teams, help break through any obstacles to that.

We hear so much about teamwork and new management styles. Is there something special about globalization that puts a premium on those skills?

It's not that globalization itself forces these new ways of working. It's that unless we change how we work, we can't make global integration a reality. We want to do two things at once. We want tight global integration in those parts of the business that don't directly face the customer—buying raw materials, working with suppliers, developing new technologies—but we also want regional autonomy and accountability in those parts of the business that do face the customer. It's not easy.

How does it work in practice?

Our North American organization is a good case study. It's a model for how we are structuring our operations around the world, and the skills required to make the new structure work.

We have a kind of three-dimensional matrix in North America today. There is a traditional organization—managers responsible for manufacturing, marketing, finance, and so on. In addition there are horizontal business teams responsible for specific products and the processes behind those products. This is where the new ways of working really matter. For example, we have a cross-functional "dishwasher team" that makes the critical decisions about our dishwasher business in North America. What are the R&D priorities? How do we position our various models relative to one another? How do we meet the needs of the key retailers? The team includes people from manufacturing, people who work with our suppliers, people from marketing, finance, the technology organization. Its charter cuts across all our U.S. dishwasher brands: KitchenAid, Whirlpool, Roper, Estate. These people come from different places, report to different bosses, worry about different problems. But they have to work together as a team.

Finally, we have brand organizations—people responsible for the integrity of all the products grouped under the Whirlpool or KitchenAid nameplates. All of our brand czars lead horizontal business teams. The brand head for Whirlpool might run the refrigerator team, for example. The brand head for Kenmore might run the oven team. That's a big change. Until recently our approach was to let our brands go head-to-head in the market, may the best brand win. Today there is more interdependence. Yes, the Whirlpool-brand czar still worries about the Whirlpool name. But he also worries about all the refrigerator brands that we make because he heads that product team. It takes a different mind-set.

How do you build this new mind-set?

You make it a priority. The Whirlpool executive committee, the company's eight senior managers, is directly responsible for the development of our top 250 people as well as the young, high-potential managers below them. We manage that talent pool on a purely global basis; whenever we think about filling an important slot, we look for people from all around the world. And we spend a lot of time on it.

We have what you might call a "human capital war room." The walls in the room are covered with the names, photographs, titles, and backgrounds of our key managers all around the world. We meet there whenever we discuss talent: Who is the best person to fill an important new assignment in Singapore? What is the right next step for one of our talented managers in Europe? How comfortable are we with our marketing team in North America?

We are much more rigorous, systematic, and forward-looking about the people equation than we were even three years ago. The Whirlpool executive committee met fourteen times last year to talk about nothing but managing the human resources of this company. That's a serious commitment.

There's more. About twenty-five miles up the road from Benton Harbor, we have spent millions of dollars to build the Whirlpool Leadership Academy. It functions as this company's university—a place where we create an integrated management capability for our people around the world. It has classrooms, satellite communications, all the latest computer technology.

Thousands of Whirlpool people cycle through this facility. We teach leadership-development courses. We teach skill-building courses in quality and customer service. We teach "one-company initiatives" designed to promote global integration. This facility is going to have a big impact on our company.

How well are these changes taking hold outside North America? How does Europe stack up?

Europe is about halfway there. They've established their business-product teams. They haven't yet identified all their cross-functional processes, but it's happening. I said earlier that the U.S. appliance industry was ahead of the rest of the world. That goes for the Whirlpool organization as well.

You have to keep in mind where we started. When we acquired Philips, we added fourteen thousand people. That's not easy. What was even tougher was that there wasn't one Philips management culture in Europe. There was a collection of cultures, many of which were at odds with others. Bauknecht, the German side of the company, had its own organization with its own headquarters. The Italian side of the business wanted nothing to do with Bauknecht. In fact, these two organizations reported to different parts of Philips's Dutch headquarters. And they marketed their brands,

27

many of which competed directly against one another, through country organizations that were independent of both Germany and Italy. Talk about
a lack of integration!

Our challenge was to integrate those distinct
businesses into one pan-European operation. But
we did not want to do it as invaders from America.
That was a big break from Philips, by the way,
which likes to send Dutch expatriates around the
world. When we bought the company, the top
twenty executives were Dutch. If you were Italian,
or French, or German, you knew you couldn't
reach the most senior level. We took a different approach. We knew we had capable people in Europe. We provided objectives, direction, and goals,
but we left it up to them to perform. And they
have.

What's it like in Europe now?

Whirlpool Europe has one and only one headquarters, in Comerio, Italy. It's like a mini–United
Nations. The top managers there speak five different languages and represent seven nationalities.
We've begun to make sense of the different
brands—Bauknecht on the high end, Whirlpool
in the middle, Ignis in the value segment—and
continue to reinforce their distinct positioning.
We've restructured manufacturing and distribution. There used to be twenty-eight warehouses
across Europe. Now there are sixteen, with plans
to shrink to nine. Our factories supply the various

brands with differentiated products, but they also share technology and components across brands.

The results speak for themselves. Philips had lost money for as far back as we looked. When we bought the business, we vowed that it would eventually earn margins comparable to what we earn in North America—about 10 percent pretax. Well, in the early 1990s, a competitive business got even more competitive, and margins in the United States fell to about 5 percent. We've built them back to 10 percent, and our margins in Europe are running at about 5 percent. We've got a way to go, but the people there have done some remarkable things.

All of which raises a dilemma that confronts so many big companies: How do you respect national differences, navigate through a world of subsidiaries, strategic alliances, and joint ventures, and still maintain one corporate culture?

You need a common strategic vision, a common set of values, a common set of performance goals, and common measures of success. People in Whirlpool speak many different languages, work in many different business cultures, have very different traditions. We can't change that, nor do we want to. But everyone has a clear sense of what we are trying to achieve and how we are supposed to get there. Not just shared values, which are important, but our core business processes—how we get things done. More important, every one of those core business processes was designed not by senior managers in Benton Harbor, but by cross-functional, cross-border teams who took ownership of them and helped drive them through the organization.

Our approach to managing quality, the Worldwide Excellence System, is our single most powerful cultural tool. We didn't just import some prepackaged quality system, and we didn't mandate it from Benton Harbor. We assembled a cross-functional team of Americans, Europeans, Canadians, and Asians and put them in charge of developing the best quality system they could. We told them they could borrow from whatever other systems they wanted—the Baldrige Award criteria here, ISO 9000 in Europe, the Deming Prize in Japan—but their job was to develop a system that met the unique needs of this company and its customers.

It took that team six months of intensive work, but the end result was a detailed and demanding management system. And this team didn't just develop the system; it also developed the training and communications materials to move the system through the organization. People still speak English, or Spanish, or Mandarin. But when it comes to performance, they all track the same indicators: brand awareness, brand loyalty, market share, defect levels, several different productivity indexes. We all know how we stack up relative to one another and to all the overall corporate goals. The Worldwide Excellence System has become a template, a shared management language.

Another system, which we call Consumer-to-Customer, or C2C, is a disciplined approach to developing new products. Here, too, we assembled a team, which we called the Group of 16, to develop that process. The members came from all over the world, and from many different functions. It took them a long time—a year. We could have done it much quicker if we had assigned a few people from Benton Harbor. But we would not have been able to tap the worldwide expertise of the company, nor would we have been able to get the buy-in that we have today. That's because the people who developed the C2C process also translated it to their regional organizations—not in terms of language, but in terms of management culture. Today Whirlpool people won't even think about proposing a new product—whether it's for $100 million or $10 million or $1 million—without going through the C2C methodology. That's true everywhere in the world. Nobody deviates.

We've spent a lot of time discussing management. Let's end on the factory floor. why should production workers in Findlay, Ohio, or LaVergne, Tennessee, support Whirlpool's globalization? Doesn't your strategy make their lives more uncertain?

At first our people didn't think it would be good for them. It didn't seem to make sense. We were successful. Why screw things up by acquiring companies in Europe or building factories in India? Today the attitude is completely different. People understand our strategy and support it. They look at our competitors, who are having all kinds of financial problems, laying off workers and managers, worrying about their balance sheets. And then they look at us. We're reporting record results. We're adding people, not cutting back. They connect the strategy with success. Everyone wants to be part of a winner. Right now, we're winning.

THE MAPMAKER

KENICHI OHMAE

Former Chairman, McKinsey & Company Japan
Managing Director,
Yokohama Consulting Group

In the waiting room of the Tokyo offices of McKinsey & Company, the walls are decorated with antique maps. Each is exquisite, drawn and printed with care, framed with precision. And each offers a completely errroneous view of the world—a view that was generally accepted at the time of its publication, yet is now regarded as a quaint artifact of an ill-informed period.

Inside the private office of Kenichi Ohmae, McKinsey's chairman in Japan at the time of our interview, the framed maps are replaced by globes, large and small, wooden and metallic, contemporary renderings of the shape of the world.

The surroundings are entirely appropriate to the man and his message. At fifty-three, Ohmae has distinguished himself as one of the world's preeminent business Mapmakers, a consultant to industries as diverse as consumer electronics, rubber, chemicals, food, telecommunications, and financial institutions, an adviser and confidant to top government officials across Asia. Ohmae's background and personal pursuits are as impressive and broad as his professional practice. He was educated at Waseda University, the Tokyo Institute of Technology, and the Massachusetts Institute of Technology, where he received a Ph.D. in nuclear engineering. Before joining McKinsey, Ohmae worked as a senior design engineer on Japan's prototype fast-breeder reactor. He is an accomplished musician and an avid scuba diver. Known as a creative and outspoken thinker, Ohmae has published thirty-nine books, which have sold more than 2 million hardback copies in Japan, making him one of that country's most influential authors.

But he is perhaps best known for his views on globalization. From his vantage post in Tokyo, Ohmae saw the coming of the global economy well before most others. "It was relatively easy for me to see," Ohmae says, "since I had to survive in an economy where the government was consistently unable to negotitate with the Americans. The problem kept being defined as exchange rates and currency. The real problem was that the old model of the economy was completely obsolete."

Ohmae's first conceptual breakthrough was his

description of the Triad: his shorthand label for a global economy in which Japan, the United States, and Western Europe each represent an equal leg. According to Ohmae's worldview, global companies need to be present in each leg of the Triad and, at the same time, to stand above the Triad and see the entire world. With his typical flair and eagerness to provoke, Ohmae declared that the ideal place on the map for companies to locate their headquarters was Anchorage, Alaska, since it was equidistant from each leg of the Triad.

From his initial insights Ohmae began to trace the logic of competition in the evolving global economy. Regions were more important than nations; companies lost their hierarchical arrangements and became networks of offices. Decentralization and democratization became the important operating principles for the new global enterprise.

Nor has Ohmae been content to offer this advice solely to corporate clients looking for strategic insights. In 1993 he published *An Ideal Country*, a book in which he outlined his prescription for a wide-ranging political revamping of Japan. The goal, Ohmae said, was to transform that country into one of the world's most livable nations. At the same time that the book appeared, Ohmae launched the Reform of the Heisei—a grass-roots political movement whose name refers to the reign of Japan's current emperor, Akihito—complete with candidates pledged to enact his platform of decentralization, deregulation, and tax reform.

In keeping with Ohmae's theories on globalization, the Reform of the Heisei envisages a Japan made up of eleven self-governing and economically viable regions, with the central government giving up most of its control over local governments. In his first electoral forays, elections for the 511-member Lower House of the Japanese Diet, 82 of the 106 candidates endorsed by Ohmae's group won their races, providing the opening salvo for the political movement. As a next step, Ohmae ran for governor of Tokyo in the 1995 election. He lost—but succeeded in raising his set of issues. Even as he continues to advise global companies on how to navigate with the new map of the world, Kenichi Ohmae has begun remaking the map of Japan.

Before we explore the new map of the world, can you describe what the old map looked like?

KENICHI OHMAE: In the old days, both countries and companies were self-sufficient and internally integrated. You had a map of individual nations, occupied by individual companies. Take a typical manufacturing organization. All the functions—production, engineering, sales and marketing, finance, personnel—existed inside the organization. All the company's strategic and product decisions were made in its home country by executives from that country. Companies exported products from their home country to other countries and sold identical products in all these "foreign" markets. The map was simple and neat.

What were the principles behind the economic model that the old map documented?

In the old model, national economies performed based on the conventional "laws" of economics. The relationship between increasing supply and increasing employment was direct and linear, which made it possible to manage national economies from the center.

The theory was simple: If demand picks up, supply picks up to meet demand and employment picks up to generate supply. It was all mechanical and predictable. Franklin Roosevelt used this model as the basis for the New Deal: The government stimulated demand, demand stimulated supply, supply created jobs. If there weren't enough jobs, the government could simply spend more money, stimulate more demand, increase supply, and create new jobs. It was an inward-looking model for an inward-looking world. Because the system was essentially closed, countries believed they could basically solve their problems inside their borders. From time to time countries might require some minor adjustments to their currency, but the fundamental economic relationships were stable and self-contained.

Unfortunately, even though that model is totally

obsolete today, many governments—and too many companies—still use it to make their decisions. Even many of those who recognize that the world has changed still try desperately to minimize the effects of that change on their thinking and planning. Rather than accept the fact that the world has an entirely different map, they operate as if they could still assume the contours of the old national model and then sprinkle in a few minor modifications.

Why is the old model obsolete?

Because it doesn't account for three fundamental changes that have overturned how the world used to work—both for companies and for governments.

The first, of course, is globalization. The closed-country model no longer applies. Companies have globalized their sources of supply. Components and finished products cross borders all around the world, all the time, which means that the old predictable, linear relationships—the assumed links between demand, supply, and jobs—no longer correspond to reality.

Let's say demand for some very hot product, laptop computers, takes off in the United States. Sure, supply increases to meet demand. But where are the new jobs created? Not in the United States. Companies like Apple and Compaq have built factories in countries like Ireland and Scotland. That's where the new jobs are created. So much for the old relationship between supply, demand, and jobs. So much for the old laws of economics.

The second change is the shift from blue-collar jobs to steel-collar jobs. When the old model was created, robots were only science fiction. When you apply that model today, it has no way of accounting for the introduction of robots or other forms of automated, information technology–driven machinery. Robots allow you to increase output, increase productivity, increase supply in response to new demand—and still reduce the human head count. What's true for robots is true for many other forms of information technology. Like globalization, information technology fundamentally changes the old economic equations.

Even so, we still see the old thinking all the time. The U.S. government announces that it wants to create more jobs. So the special trade representative flies to Japan and insists, "You, the Japanese government, must stimulate your economy. If you import more of our products, it will help us create more American jobs." Japan stimulates its economy and boosts imports from America. Only jobs in America still go down. Why? Because American companies are smart. They respond to the increased demand not by adding workers, but by adding robots and investing in information technology or by increasing production in Mexico and Korea. Output goes up, but jobs may even go down. The link between increased supply and new jobs has been fundamentally broken.

In fact, one reason why many Japanese companies have been so competitive in so many industries is that they have made this shift from blue-collar to steel-collar workers. Other countries, especially those in Europe, have resisted the shift in the name of preserving jobs. And they do have plenty of employment—for a while. But what they gain in short-term jobs they lose in long-term competitiveness. Inevitably they lose first the jobs, then the companies, and finally the industries.

The third change that undermines the old model is the rise of the service sector and the serviceware economy. The old economy was geared almost exclusively to manufacturing. Everybody's goal was to make more manufactured goods—more cars, more furniture, more steel, more of all kinds of tangible things. Now the balance in the economy is shifting. Today we're seeing the rise of services everywhere. Today services based on knowledge are the greatest source of new value. If you look at manufacturing and service companies in both Japan and the United States, you'll see the same pattern: Companies in the service sector have overtaken companies in manufacturing. Microsoft, Nintendo, and Sega all have a higher stock-market value than General Motors.

Nintendo is a powerful example. It has annual sales of $5 billion, has made annual profits of as much as $1.5 billion, but has only eight hundred employees. Many government officials would see so few jobs as a problem. But at a corporate tax rate of 50 percent, Nintendo contributes $750 million in taxes every year to Japan. Is that a problem?

Of course, many people in the United States still argue about the need to maintain a manufacturing base. Can you build a healthy economy around video games?

The problem in the United States is that you get confused between two different kinds of jobs in the service sector. One kind is in the intellectual service sector. This is knowledge work, producing innovations that come from new ideas and new technologies. It could be creating video games or powerful business software or designing and engineering new products. This is real work that creates real value and generates a rising standard of living.

The other kind is service jobs such as flipping hamburgers and making beds. These jobs are low-wage; they're the kind everybody is afraid of. But if people saw the world correctly, they'd understand the difference. They'd appreciate the critical importance of the intellectual service sector. Unfortunately, government officials and economists don't help. They don't see the distinction, because they themselves are still stuck in the old world, where all that matters is manufacturing.

What too many people still fail to see is the shift in how and where value is created today. Let's say manufacturing development goes to China or Mexico. That's fine if it's relatively simple, low-end assembly work. That's where it belongs. The strong, developed countries absolutely have the ability to re-create and rejuvenate themselves with companies like Nintendo and Microsoft. These are the companies that invent and innovate.

But don't economic statistics indicate that manufacturing is still the backbone of a nation's economy?

Economic statistics are notoriously unreliable. Even as industrialized economies are shifting to services, we're losing our ability to track these economies and this shift. Take customs offices, for example. They are completely out of touch with most knowledge-based transactions. In fact, the more technologically advanced, higher value-added the transaction, the less likely it is that government tracking systems will be able to account for it, or even know about it. National economic membranes are not only permeable; they're practically transparent.

What happens when Lotus sells its Lotus 1-2-3 spreadsheet to a company in Japan? Lotus doesn't ship hundreds of copies on floppy disks for the customs office to record. It ships one master copy to Japan, its Japanese subsidiary reproduces it by the thousands, and then the customer installs it on thousands or even millions of computers. But that's not what the customs office sees. Its numbers show that Lotus shipped one copy to Japan. In fact, it doesn't even need to ship it. Lotus can send the software electronically, through the telephone lines.

Let's talk about the new map. What has globalization done to the map of the world as viewed by CEOs and strategists?

The map continues to evolve. On the old map, which was accurate right up into the 1970s, each country had very distinct borders. In the early 1980s, as globalization began to erase those borders, you saw a map of the world with Japan, Western Europe, and the United States as the three dominant bodies. These three centers were what we dubbed the Triad, and that's what people meant by globalization. Companies with a presence in Japan, Western Europe, and the United States considered themselves global competitors.

Today we're seeing that map transform itself into two different sets of maps. First, membership in the Triad is changing: It's no longer just the major countries. There is a more elaborate set of players within each of the three areas.

The third leg of the Triad, for example, used to be limited to Japan. Today it has expanded to include the entire Pacific region, because so many other countries have caught up. The perspective has changed in the Americas as well. Canada and Mexico are now important markets in the Triad; it's not just the United States anymore. In Europe the map is changing, too; the eastern border has blurred. So while the importance of being a major player inside the Triad is the same, the borders of the Triad itself have changed to encompass new members.

What's the second change in the map?

The second change involves details within each leg of the Triad. As national borders have disappeared, region-states have emerged. This is a huge shift. Today a major global player will be much better off forgetting which nations are in the Triad and instead addressing key markets by regions. I believe there are thirty key economic regions in the world today. If you are strong in them, you can reach 80 percent of the global demand for products and services.

In Europe, for example, it makes little sense to talk about Germany or France as markets anymore. Your company really wants to produce and sell in an integrated regional market—the one that stretches from Strasbourg to Bavaria, for instance. It's not France, it's not Germany. It's a region that represents the vital center of Europe.

That's true in each leg of the Triad. More than ever, the relevant geographic units aren't countries. They are clusters of regions governed by economies of service and economies of scale in information. China today is not a single economic nation; it already consists of six "region states."

But it could easily disaggregate into something like twenty-eight Singapore-sized economic regions.

What are these economies of scale?

Electronic borders are replacing physical borders. And it is these electronic borders that define distinct consumer markets. Let me give you an example from Japan. There really isn't any national television broadcasting in Japan. We do have a national broadcasting system, but as far as advertisements are concerned, you can't automatically run ads across the country. People in Osaka may see them, but people in Tokyo won't. Which means, for consumer products, that the "Japanese market" is really a set of markets defined by the electronic boundaries of where your ads can run.

That's just an example. Today there is no such thing as a true pan-American strategy or pan-European strategy or pan-Asian strategy. When you look at the thirty key regions, it turns out that the most efficient size for an economic unit at the regional level is between 5 million and 20 million people. Five million is the absolute minimum size; 20 million is the most efficient. Once you reach that scale, the region not only shares electronic communication, it also typically has both a major-league airport and a harbor that are interconnected to the rest of the world. It reaches economies of scale in both services and information.

Do these thirty regions act in more or less similar ways, or are there big differences among them?

You can draw a map of the world based on the per capita GNP of the population and use it as a guide for corporate strategy. For example, all over the world, before a country or region reaches the $5,000 per capita GNP level, more than 50 percent of its people's income goes just to buy food. That leaves very little in the way of disposable income.

Once a country passes the $5,000 per capita GNP level, both religion and military adventurism become declining industries. National borders begin to go down as people start looking for items that are the best and the cheapest from anywhere in the world. They begin to select products based on brand rather than rampant nationalistic feelings. All over the world they become unwilling to say, "I'll buy American" or "I'll buy Japanese," just to help improve the balance of trade statistics.

Then at $10,000 it's such a clear trend that, as a corporation, unless you recognize it, you will both miss opportunities and, ultimately, threaten your own existence. In Asia alone look at the number of countries that have recently joined the $10,000 club. Singapore is over $12,000, Hong Kong is at $14,000, Australia is at $14,000, and Taiwan is just over $10,000. Amazingly, the customers in each of these countries all behave the same way once they cross that $10,000 per capita line. Their educational levels, their academic and cultural backgrounds, their lifestyles all become more and more homogeneous. At the $10,000 level, people—wherever they are—have access to the same information, and that information adds further to the degree of homogeneity. People start behaving in very similar ways. Because of this information era, with common knowledge of brands and goods, everyone knows what's in fashion. They start to become global consumers.

As this happens, companies that try to differentiate customers according to their national differences will be left out in the cold. There are already 700 million people in the world who are members of the $10,000 club. Companies that look for commonalities among this 700 million will be able to take advantage of economies of scale to amortize their fixed-cost investments and appeal to global consumers. That's critical.

What's so critical about economies of scale and fixed costs?

The shift in the mid-1980s from variable to fixed costs in the nature of competition is one of the most important aspects of globalization. Take research and development. In Japan we used to license innovations from companies in the United States or Europe. A Japanese company would pay, say, 2 percent of its sales as a royalty. If sales went up, the royalty went up. It was a variable cost. Then, in the mid-1980s, as global competition intensified, foreign companies refused to give Japanese companies licenses. So these companies had to spend huge amounts of money to innovate for themselves.

Suddenly R&D became a fixed cost. You had to get hundreds of people to work on it. You had to establish research labs and development centers. The same was true for other parts of every company. Manufacturing used to be labor-intensive—again a variable cost. But increasingly, as a result of global competition, companies switched to robots, automation, steel-collar systems. That's a fixed cost: You've made a capital investment in production technology that doesn't change with volumes.

It's an interactive process. Global competition was one of the major forces driving the change from variable to fixed costs. At the same time, once companies made the switch, it made sense to produce for the whole world.

Let's turn from maps to management. How would you describe the challenge of being a global company today?

The essence of being a global company is to maintain a kind of tension within the organization without being undone by it. Some companies say the new world requires homogeneous products—one size fits all everywhere. Others say the world requires endless customization—special products for every region. The best global companies understand it's neither and it's both. They keep the two perspectives in mind simultaneously.

Global companies need to be completely at home in each leg of the Triad. They need to be deeply rooted in the special characteristics of each leg of the Triad, have talent in each leg, understand the local market conditions in each leg. At the same time they need to stand above the Triad and see the world as a whole. They need to understand how consumers everywhere—above the $10,000 per capita level—are essentially the same, despite local tastes and preferences.

How does adopting this "double vision" change the way companies do business?

It certainly changes the way they organize their operations. At the highest level, companies need a global superstructure—an organization that looks at the entire world as a single unit. The major responsibility of this organization is to make sure that work is located where it can best be done and that information and products cross borders efficiently. The point is to eliminate redundant investment and to share information.

For example, if Japan is very good at R&D for electronic components, then the superstructural organization would locate that R&D in Japan and make sure the components can easily cross the borders of the Triad. The superstructure is there to place the initial investments in the most opportune locations and to coordinate cross-border movements.

If the top level of the organization exists as a superstructure above nations, what exists below the superstructure?

Go back to what I said about regions. Below the superstructure that's the level that makes sense. Again, take Japan as an example. When most foreign companies come to Japan, they set up a national base in Tokyo. It makes sense, right? Tokyo is the capital. There are 33 million people in the Tokyo metropolitan area, with a GNP practically the size of France. Tokyo must be the right place to enter—or at least everyone thinks so. But what happens when foreign companies locate in Tokyo? They immediately meet tough competition. They get lost in the hustle and bustle. They never get noticed. Instead they get exhausted, and they never reach the Japan beyond Tokyo.

What if you think about Japan not as one nation but as a collection of different regions? The Kansai region based in Osaka is a fantastic point of entry to the Japanese market. It has 22 million people, about the population of Canada. If Kansai were a country, it would be a member of the G-7. The new Kansai airport has direct flights all over the world. It's not only a terrific place to build a regional market for Japan, it's also a wonderful place to have an Asian headquarters. There's also

Hokkaido. It has 6 million people, about the size of Switzerland. If you're a foreign company trying to enter Japan, is 6 million people not a worthwhile market in which to begin? Or what about Kyushu? It's roughly the same size as Korea. Again, if you're a foreign company, isn't that big enough?

Does this notion of organizing by region apply only to Japan, or does it work for other countries as well?

It works the same when I talk with Japanese companies about going to the United States. I always tell them, "Don't go to the 'United States.' Don't even think about the United States as one country. When you go to the United States, you have to go to a region in the United States. Go to Orange County in California. Go to Atlanta in the Southeast. Go to the Pacific Northwest: Portland, Seattle, Vancouver in British Columbia. Go to the Dallas–Fort Worth region in Texas. But don't go to this big, undifferentiated United States."

When you begin to think this way, you redraw the map of the United States into loose regional associations that cross more familiar borders. You can think of a Great Lakes region that includes Toronto on the Canadian side and then crosses the border to include Detroit, Cleveland, Chicago, and the major industrial cities of the U.S. Midwest.

If I had a high-quality industrial product and I

wanted to bring my company into the large market of the United States, I would choose that as my first target market. If that is the region that has the highest concentration of industrial companies, I would want my company to be part of that market. It would have companies I could do business with, a high concentration of skilled industrial workers, a large number of smart customers. If I had an industrial product, it wouldn't matter that no one in San Antonio or Las Vegas knew me. I would focus on the Great Lakes region as my point of entry.

So far your description of the new global organization has a superstructure at the level of the Triad and regions beneath that. Where does that leave old-fashioned country organizations?

Once you begin to see the world as a superstructure above and regions below, the only troublesome part is the unit in between—this thing called the nation-state. That's the unit for which statistics are collected, around which people form their political emotions, and where conflicts occur. It's also a unit that is obsolete. For economic purposes, nation-states have become unnatural, even dysfunctional.

The outmoded unit of "the nation" makes it much harder for business leaders to make sound, informed choices about their strategies and organizations. If you're in business today, all you can get are national statistics. They can tell you Canadian output, American output, Mexican output. But if you want an accurate picture of the way economies really work, or how your organization should work, you have to assemble your own data on regional output. That makes it harder to make decisions.

Here's an example. Even before the passage of the North American Free Trade Agreement, the region from Texas to California along the border between the United States and Mexico had already become incredibly attractive as a location for assembly industries such as electronics, automobiles, and their components. But as far as the data are concerned, that region doesn't even exist. To get an accurate understanding of this vibrant, cohesive regional economy, you have to combine numbers on southern California with data on Tijuana, and numbers on northeastern Mexico with data on southern Texas.

It sounds like the notion of global and regional organizations makes it more complicated than ever for executives to manage their companies.

It's a lot simpler than people make it. If you're an American CEO, just imagine that you're the astronaut Neil Armstrong, who looked down from space and said that there were no borders on the planet Earth. That's a healthy perspective. You should spend some time orienting yourself to the global business sphere in which you operate.

But then you need to look harder. You should

ask yourself, What do I see that is familiar? What do I recognize? What can I identify? This is what I call the zebra effect. From a distance you might call a zebra a gray horse. When you get close enough, you can see the distinct black and white stripes. A good CEO has to get close enough to see the distinct stripes.

In other words, a CEO has to look at the entire global economy and then put the company's resources where they will capture the biggest market share of the most attractive regions. Perhaps as you draw closer from outer space you see a region around the Pacific Northwest, near Puget Sound, that is vibrant and prosperous. Then you recognize the region stretching from New York to Boston that is still doing awful. You might see a booming concentration of computer companies and software publishers around Denver, and similar concentrations around Dallas–Fort Worth. Along the coast of California and in parts of New England you will see regions that are strong centers for health care and biotechnology. As a CEO, that's where you put your resources and shift your emphasis.

Once companies have shifted their focus from nations to regions, what comes next?

The real test is to show favoritism. You have to make choices, region by region, not country by country, about where you want to invest. You have to have the strategic courage to pick your spots and stick with them. You have to think about the sequence of development on a region-by-region basis.

These choices differ based on the company and the situation. When you are starting out, when you want to learn from your first market experiments, you have to eliminate the extreme cases. That even means eliminating extreme successes, which may make you look and feel good but don't really teach you anything useful. For example, you may be able to succeed in Texas with a new product, but it may be so well suited to Texas that it doesn't tell you much about whether it would sell elsewhere. On the other hand, if you succeed in some other location, say Salt Lake City, that success may be more meaningful—and thus more repeatable. So you want to start in Salt Lake City.

If executives follow your strategic advice, where does it lead in terms of how they organize their companies?

If you build your company region by region, almost automatically you end up with a networked approach to the organization. It's not unlike the way a consulting firm is organized. When a consulting firm talks about growing, it almost never talks about "entering a country." It talks about opening a new office in Melbourne or Sydney, not "competing in Australia." It thinks about opening in Toronto and Montreal, not "building a business in Canada." Likewise, consulting firms don't have a hierarchy among their offices. They may have a headquarters, but the job of headquarters is not to control the offices but to support the needs of the regional offices. The same kind of model applies to more and more companies.

What does this say about the future role of head-quarters?

The role of a headquarters is that of a catalyst, a lubricant. It helps establish a common value system for the company. It distributes new information and cross-fertilizes knowledge as quickly as possible from one region to another. What's the best product or service developed in a particular region? What's the newest discovery? What's the best practice? Headquarters provides quick feedback and allows the whole system to learn, respond, and maintain its balance. Actually, I'm encouraging companies to stop thinking about headquarters altogether. It makes more sense to think about the company's residence. You don't really need a headquarters today, except for legal or financial-reporting purposes. The more important question is where you have your residence for creative purposes.

What's a corporate residence?

Your residence is where you are most at home and where there is a concentration of companies like yours. Your residence needs to have a certain ambiance; it needs to be where the action is for your industry. That's where you put your creative people. For example, for financial, marketing, and distribution purposes, movie companies need to put their numbers people in New York. But the creative side needs to have its residence in Hollywood. You can find those kinds of concentrations in most any industry—Boston and San Diego for biotechnology, New York and Milan for design.

If you do away with the idea of a headquarters, what happens to the distinction between domestic and foreign operations?

In this kind of organization, there's no such thing as "foreign" or "domestic." Everybody is domestic and the organization is global. That's the most important, enlightened value system you eventually reach. In a flat, networked organization, the person in charge of Osaka is as important as the person in charge of Tokyo, who's as important as the person in charge of Milan or Rome. Ideas travel across the network among peers. You don't go by hierarchy. People from the different regions get together often enough so that they know one another—they have a family feeling.

Eventually, when people get together, chances are that if one person from one region starts a conversation by saying, "I think it's time for us to change our strategy," about 70 percent of the other people will say, "I was thinking the same thing," and all will agree to set up a cross-regional task force. The challenge could be anything—downsizing, a shift from hardware to software, a move into cleaning up the environment. As long as there are empowered regional management teams, the company can react very quickly.

Do you see any examples of this approach today?

American companies are beginning to move in this direction, but usually it happens when they get as far away from the United States as possible. Back in the United States, they'll have their headquarters in New York, Los Angeles, or Minneapolis, and the company will have a typical hierarchical structure. But when they decide to come to Asia, perhaps to China, and begin to see regionalization in its most embryonic phase, they organize themselves differently.

The question usually is, Where should we locate our Chinese headquarters? Well, Shanghai is as important as Guangdong. Tianjin is as important as Beijing. Of course, it depends on what you want to do. If you're talking about chemicals, you need to look at the Shangdong Peninsula. If it's electronics assembly, it may be the Liaodong Peninsula. This discussion will be going on and suddenly someone will say, "You know, maybe we need to look at China as five or six separate regions."

Pretty soon you redraw the map. Hong Kong is

already the capital of the province of Guangdong; it is to Guangdong what Los Angeles is to Orange County. And Shanghai is essentially the East Coast headquarters site for China—it's like New York. All of a sudden, Americans gain a better understanding of China, and they structure their companies to reflect that.

If companies no longer see their operations in terms of foreign and domestic, what happens to relationships between companies and their national governments?

Increasingly, as corporations become more global, they will simply choose to avoid bad governments. Governments will no longer be able to decide which companies or industries to favor. Companies will decide where to locate and which government they will work with. Companies will rate their governments. They will vote with their resources and investments.

Companies are no longer products of one nation. They may have been born in a certain country, but they're not married to that country permanently. There is really very little left that ties a company to the place of its birth. The only umbilical cord is the location of the headquarters. And if the regulatory authorities of the headquarters country are nasty, the headquarters is simply gone.

Are there any examples?

We have one here in Japan. Yoahan, a major supermarket, has moved its headquarters to Hong Kong. Japanese laws regulating the creation of new supermarkets and hypermarkets give a huge advantage to incumbents. It takes ten years to get approval to open a new supermarket. Yoahan decided it wasn't worth it and moved out. The company has since become the largest retailer on the southern coast of China. It's now growing on the East Coast of the United States.

Perhaps the country that has seen this happen the most is Sweden. For decades the Swedish government created a political and social environment that was inhospitable to business. What happened? Companies like ABB, Tetra-Pak, and Nobel—big, multibillion-dollar operations—simply packed up and moved their headquarters to Switzerland. In today's world, companies can choose their governments.

What's the biggest threat to the continued emergence of the global economy?

Unless we educate the economists, the bureaucrats, and the politicians, unless we teach them what the real world is all about and help them unlearn the old model, we'll see growing conflict between the leading edge of business and the trailing or protected part of business. We'll have leading-edge companies pushing to get to the twenty-first century and the rest of the system left in the eighteenth. The result will be huge disparities, not only among companies, but, more important, among countries or whole regions of the world.

The more we cling to obsolete, wrongheaded interpretations of competition, the longer we retain maps and economic models that no longer fit the facts, the more we'll see protected industries rewarded for not making an inch of progress and leading-edge companies penalized for making bold moves. We'll see companies pushed back home, having to give up the process of globalization, because every time they make progress, that progress itself becomes a new problem. Unless we can drive this process of education, we are in for some painful and difficult times.

THE FIRST MATE

BARBARA KUX

Vice-President, Nestlé S.A.

There's the story of how, for weeks, angry protesters from IG Metall, the powerful German trade union, blocked her from entering the headquarters of the manufacturing company she was working to restructure.

There's the story of how she negotiated the first, biggest, and most successful joint venture in Poland, and then had to watch as the government minister she negotiated with resigned because of the backlash the deal generated.

There's the story of how she persuaded a commercial airliner to wait nervously in Zagreb while one of her executives raced to the airport to escape the civil war in Yugoslavia.

Taken separately, each of these stories is like an entry in a manager's diary of life in the new global economy. Taken together, they make a broader and more important point: In a world stocked with grand theories of global competition, where CEOs and strategists search for the next big strategic idea, companies also need managers with the self-confidence to live by their wits—people who can move quickly, cut through resistance, and do what it takes to create change across borders.

So don't think of Barbara Kux as one of the rising stars in European business—although, as a high-ranking line manager at Nestlé at age forty-two, she certainly is that. And don't think of her as one of the toughest-minded competitors any-where—although, as the young executive who locked up Eastern Europe's power-generation business for ABB (Asea Brown Boveri), the Swedish-Swiss electrical-equipment giant, she is that, too. Think of her instead as a resilient First Mate in the management revolution sweeping Eastern Europe and the world.

First as president of ABB Power Ventures, now as the Nestlé vice-president responsible for Eastern Europe and the former Soviet Union (a market of 400 million consumers), Barbara Kux has spent the last six years living by her wits: finding young, local managers who can lead project teams and motivate people, teaching them what she knows, assembling experts on finance, quality, and marketing to teach what they know, and delivering results faster than anyone thought possible. Working

on a continent that seems overwhelmed by economic malaise, political drift, and ethnic violence,
she remains determined and confident: a change
agent delivering on the promise of globalization.

Kux, who was born in Zurich, signed on with
ABB in September 1989, as the political rumblings
in Eastern Europe were turning into an earth-
quake. She had spent all of one week in the region—in Prague, as a tourist—spoke none of the
languages, knew little of the politics. But she had
made a mark as a young management consultant
working to restructure ABB's German operations,
so the company's top executives asked her to try
something even harder. She got a small office in
Zurich, half a secretary, and a three-part mission:
to make ABB a "true insider" in the region, to do
so ahead of the company's giant rivals, and to turn
the companies she acquired into world-class operations.

In just three years, Kux negotiated five joint-
venture deals for companies in Poland, Hungary,
and the former Yugoslavia. Those operations,
which collectively employ nearly eight thousand
people, were all losing money when Kux acquired
them. All but one were solidly profitable when she
left in late 1992. In fact, all but one were profitable
within the first year of the joint venture.

Kux began her current assignment with Nestlé
on January 1, 1993. She no longer worries about
turbines, boilers, and transmission gear. Instead
the issues are: Which of Nestlé's chocolate factories in the East can meet world-class standards?

What blends of Nescafé are right for Poland? How can Nestlé improve the soups it makes in Hungary? The game is still young, but Kux is convinced that the principles and techniques perfected during her three years at ABB are directly relevant to causing change on behalf of the largest food company in the world.

In the new global economy, everyone agrees that ideas are the most important business asset. Barbara Kux is in the messy business of turning ideas into results.

CEOs everywhere are searching for global managers. They know the world is changing, they know their people need new skills, but they're not sure what those skills are or how to teach them. What are the defining traits of a global manager?

BARBARA KUX: The first trait of a global manager is to be nimble. Move fast but don't hipshoot. Do some analysis, but not too much analysis, and then act. The problem with many of the Swiss and German companies I know is that they analyze themselves to death. When they evaluate an investment in a new country, for example, they ask for projections out to the third decimal point instead of saying, "Okay, there are three things I have to know about this investment, and once I know them, then I move." Maybe you're not always right. That's okay. It's better to be 70 percent right and move fast than to be perfect and wait. Speed is a plus in global business.

The second trait is self-confidence. Where other people see risks, global managers see opportunity. The first deal I did for ABB was a joint venture with a Polish company called Zamech, a turbine manufacturer in Elblag, near Gdansk. This was a big deal. It was a giant, inefficient plant—there were nearly five thousand workers at the time— making complex, expensive products. A gas turbine can sell for as much as $100 million when you include all the engineering and installation costs. At the time, this was Poland's first major joint venture with a Western company. Not only that, but there was no law in Poland for how to set up a joint venture. No one in the government could make a decision because there were no laws to guide them.

Lots of companies, understandably I suppose, said, "There's no legal basis to do a joint venture or make an acquisition. Let's wait." We said, "There's no legal basis to do a joint venture? Great! We'll go in there first and create the legal basis." We saw it as an opportunity rather than a risk. That willingness to take risks is a function of self-confidence.

Are there other traits?

Modesty is an important one. Global managers must avoid the colonialist mentality—"We know best." You have to let the people on the scene, the local managers, make change in their organizations. That's one of the great strengths of Nestlé, with its hundred-year tradition of delegating power to the regions rather than centralizing power at headquarters in Vevey. A typical German company in the United States still has Germans at the top. A Japanese company anywhere has Japanese managers. When General Electric bought Tungsram, the light-bulb manufacturer in Hungary, it sent an expatriate from Canada to run the operation. I think that was a mistake. Why can't the people there change things?

The last trait I would mention is that global managers are flexible and pragmatic. Many of the managers I know still plan their lives weeks or months in advance: "Six weeks from now I will be in Paris." But the business world changes so fast—especially when you do business in a place like Eastern Europe—that you can't make those kinds of plans. Or if you do make them, you have to be willing to throw them out the window the moment events demand it. Change your flight, change your schedule. If you are supposed to be in Paris, but it's better to be in Prague, go to Prague. Too many managers are so hierarchical and structured. You've got to be pragmatic.

Can you give me a sense, based on your own work, of how these traits make a difference in global business?

In mid-1989, right after Eastern Europe opened up, Percy Barnevik, the CEO of ABB, went to

Poland. He sized up the situation, determined that ABB could create a presence there, and decided to hire someone to make it happen. The company chose me; it could have been someone else. But they made one person responsible for making this happen—clear accountability. They gave me a small office, half a secretary, and a stack of documents about two possible acquisitions in Poland.

I could have spent months buried in my office reviewing those documents and studying what to do. Instead we assembled a small team. I told them we were going to move fast on these deals. I put them and me under heavy pressure: "We aren't going to analyze and negotiate for ten months." We gave ourselves two weeks. We made something like forty or fifty different business plans—a whole range of scenarios just to get a feel for what were reasonable expectations about this business. And then that was it. We decided to put in our bid for Zamech.

Then I went to the Minister of Privatization in Poland. I told him that we should form a working group of his lawyers and our lawyers to make the deal happen. We gave the group one week to reach an agreement. They took longer than a week, but we did get it done very quickly.

I signed on with ABB in September 1989. We had an agreement in principle with Zamech three months later. The new company opened for business on May 1, 1990. It is still the largest Western joint venture in Poland. And it has been a big success.

Our competitors were more cautious. If, say,

General Electric had moved aggressively into Eastern Europe, they might have posed a major strategic challenge in Europe. But they chose not to do that. Today, if any of ABB's competitors wanted a production base in Eastern Europe, they would have to build it from scratch—greenfield sites. That's almost impossible.

That's the upside of being nimble. But perhaps the Zamech deal would have worked even better had you taken more time, done more analysis, negotiated more cautiously.

More time would not have changed a thing. If you have a team of analysts and you tell them, "Okay, we have two weeks to make every scenario we can think of," they will put into that exercise exactly the same effort as if you told them they had two months. Nobody can predict the future in a region as volatile as Eastern Europe—or in most regions, for that matter. What you want to know is, "Do I have a reasonable feel for the situation?" And then you move. It's really a question of self-confidence. Most companies and managers over-analyze because they lack confidence. Global managers say, "That's enough. Sure, there are risks. Let's move."

That's a nice description of the style of a global manager. But where do these people come from? What specific skills do they need?

There are certain hard skills you have to have. In Europe you have to be fluent in English and at least one more language. I speak German, English, French, and a bit of Dutch. You have to be mobile. You have to be able to travel, you have to like to travel, you have to know how to travel. I go to Eastern Europe about once a week, and I spend two or three days per visit. It's a taxing schedule. If you're not good at it, you won't make it as a global manager.

But that's just the beginning. What it really takes is a particular mind-set. I've always thought that the people who succeed as global managers are capable of mastering a whole collection of paradoxes. You have to be a strategist and an activist—to understand your company's strategic position in Asia and make an opportunistic move in Russia. You have to be a generalist and a specialist—to understand the big picture about how, say, Nestlé stacks up against Philip Morris, and the technical details about why customers in Poland prefer certain blends of coffee. You have to have a national focus and a global perspective. If you are stationed in Switzerland, you have to understand the intricacies of the Swiss capital markets. But you also have to understand the major trends in world finance and how they might change things in Switzerland. And maybe most important, you have to be a leader and a diplomat—to be tough enough to get things done, but to have a genuine social competence and conscience.

That's certainly a tall order. Can you teach that mind-set?

I don't think so. The single most important reality of working in the global economy is constant change: Politicians come and go, currencies fluctuate, information moves quickly, consumer tastes evolve, joint ventures and acquisitions reshape the playing field. The only way managers can prepare themselves for such rapid-fire change is to constantly introduce change into their own lives—to seek out different environments, different functions, different companies, different industries. Technical competence isn't good enough anymore. A global manager has to be more than a great marketer or a smart financier. You need a multidimensional background—not just for the hard skills you acquire, but for what you experience in different settings.

Does that apply to your own career?

I am not a "routine" manager. As soon as a business becomes routine, my job is finished. That's why I came to Nestlé. When I signed on with ABB, I had spent one week in Eastern Europe—in Prague, as a tourist. By the end of 1992, I felt like my job was done. With one or two exceptions, we had taken over every company in the power-generating business in the region—five joint ventures altogether, employing more than eight thousand people. And with the exception of one plant, those companies were on their way to performing at world-class standards. They had reached cruising altitude. They were making money. Solid local managers were in place. It was time for something new.

And what I'm doing at Nestlé is new: some new countries, although I still spend a lot of time in Poland, new products, new issues around consumer marketing, advertising, a new and different corporate culture. The way to be comfortable causing change is to introduce change in your own life and career.

Let's talk about the nitty-gritty process of causing change across borders. Your work in Eastern Europe has involved two very different worlds: heavy electrical equipment like gas turbines, and consumer products like chocolate, coffee, and soups. Have any common lessons emerged?

The issue isn't turbines or chocolates. The issue is productivity. In Eastern Europe we are working to get higher productivity from people and capital, more of a customer focus, and better quality across the board. Those issues are inherent to the region, not to specific industries. What goes for turbines basically goes for chocolates or just about any other product you can name.

Now, obviously, there are some differences—sales and distribution are very different, to say the least, for chocolates versus turbines. With heavy electrical equipment, you don't have the same need for local customization that you have with consumer products. At ABB we wanted huge economies of scale across borders. The goal was to build as many products in as few factories as possible. Consumer products are less capital-intensive, and you want more local production so you can accommodate local tastes. Nestlé has nearly five hundred factories around the world. In a way the management challenge here is more complex than at ABB, even if the products seem more simple. With Nestlé, there's just not the same capacity to do things the same way globally.

But the management similarities far outweigh the differences. The restructuring needs in Eastern Europe are the same. And so is the potential. You can make dramatic improvements in Eastern Europe, and you can make them quickly. But there are no formulas; you can't copy what you do in the West. And there are no routines; you can't fall off your chair when things change. In my world, things change all the time. You have to be pragmatic enough to deal with it.

What do Western companies do wrong when they cross borders into a region like Eastern Europe?

For one thing, they get too fancy. So many companies make an acquisition in Eastern Europe and immediately add powerful new computers, intricate new control systems, all the latest technology. What you really need is much more simple. You need good phone lines so you can exchange data and know what's happening on the scene. You need to teach people a common language—English—so you can communicate with them. You need a nice hotel so the outside experts who visit and teach can be comfortable. If it's too difficult to get to a factory in Eastern Europe or too miserable to stay there, advisers will find lots of reasons not to go.

The second big mistake is that they insist on doing things themselves. That's arrogant as well as unproductive. When we went into Eastern Europe, we made two points. First, we would not send in a "rescue team" from Switzerland to save the companies. It would be up to the Poles or the Hungarians or the Czechs to solve their own problems. Second, we would not make a "discount" for Eastern Europe. We expected these companies to be just as productive as their counterparts in the West, and we expected their managers to turn them around quickly. Sure, we provided lots of training and technical support, more than if we had acquired a company in Indiana or Italy. But we expected our local managers to drive the change. And they did.

Like so much in business, bringing about change is really a question of selecting the right people. Good managers in Eastern Europe are just as smart as good managers in America or Japan. And I really believe that good managers are born, not made. Every manager needs some basic skills: accounting, finance, marketing. You can teach those skills. But you can't teach initiative, creativity, passion, vision. You have to find the right people, trust them, let them do the work.

Can you give us a sense of what's possible?

The best example is Zamech, which is still one of the most successful joint ventures I've been involved with. The negotiations weren't easy. The Poles had seen what GE paid for Tungsram. They knew about the resources Volkswagen was prepared to pump into Skoda Works, the Czech auto manufacturer. So our first job was to bring them down to earth. We commissioned Ernst & Young to do a clearheaded valuation. Both sides negotiated hard and we made a fair deal. ABB bought 76 percent of the equity, we gave 5 percent to the workers, and the Polish government held on to 19 percent.

The new company opened for business in May 1990. The first thing we did was to put an infrastructure in place—the pragmatic steps I talked about earlier. We started intensive language training right away, to get people talking in English. We opened "Hotel Zamech," a little place that we rented and renovated, in June. We established a satellite link between Elblag and ABB headquarters in Zurich in August. Once we had the infrastructure, we could begin to design a comprehensive change program.

What were the basic elements of that program?

It was built on four core principles. I know them well, because the program we developed for Zamech was exactly what we used with our other operations in Poland, as well as in Hungary and Croatia.

First, we reorganized the operations into profit centers with well-defined budgets, strict performance targets, and clear lines of authority and accountability. Next, we identified a core group of change agents from local management—we called them our "hungry wolves"—and created small teams responsible for eleven high-priority programs, from reorganizing and retraining the sales force to slashing total cycle time and redesigning the factory layout. Third, we transferred ABB expertise from around the world to support the hungry wolves, without interfering with their work or running their programs. And finally, we kept standards high and expected quick results. We set very demanding targets.

And the Poles were able to deliver on all this?

Absolutely. The management team we put in place lacked all the standard business tools we take for granted in the West. They didn't know what cash flow was, they didn't understand much about marketing, their ideas about customer service were rather limited. But their ambition was incredible. You could feel their hunger to excel. When we began the talent search, we told our Zamech contacts that we wanted to see the thirty people they would take along tomorrow if they were going to open their own business. That's who we got, and they turned out to be remarkable.

The managing director of Zamech, a man named Pawel Olechnowicz, is about my age. At the time we finalized the joint venture, he was a third-level manager in the castings department, a very junior guy. He had been elected managing director by the workers just before the takeover, but he didn't know us and we didn't know him. He came to Zurich to present himself. He was dressed very plainly. We weren't sure what to make of him, but after listening to his presentation we decided to trust him. Today he is one of the best managers anywhere in the world for ABB. He learned English in two months. He learned the basics of finance. He is a very charismatic leader, which is why the workers chose him in the first place. We made the right decision.

But are ambition and charisma enough, especially in Eastern Europe? Don't local managers need hard business skills?

We designed a very intensive program to introduce our hungry wolves to basic business concepts and to help them transfer these concepts down through the ranks. It was sort of a mini-MBA. It was a big deal. The program covered five mod-

ules—business strategy, marketing, finance, manufacturing, and human resources—and was taught
by faculty members of INSEAD, the top French
business school. The sessions ran from Thursday
evenings to Saturday noon. We used Western business school cases, which we translated into Polish.
We held the sessions in Warsaw, in the press brief-
ing room of the prime minister's office, which had
the best facilities for simultaneous translation. We
used five translators to help keep the discussions
moving.

I was very worried when we started the mini-
MBA. I spoke at a lunch to open the first session,
but then I left. I didn't want to interfere. The next
morning, after I got back to Switzerland, I just had
to know how things were going. I called the press
room and got the INSEAD professor who was running the program. He was ecstatic. "We're in the
middle of Caterpillar versus Komatsu," he told me.
That's a famous Harvard Business School case.
"And the quality of the analysis, the content of the
presentations, is excatly what you would expect
from business students anywhere in the world." At
that point I knew we were on our way.

What's the bottom line of the change program?

By the end of 1992 the changes at Zamech had
really taken hold. And the results were pretty remarkable. Revenue had more than doubled compared with 1990. Profits had more than tripled. In

fact, Zamech today is one of the most profitable business units in all of ABB. Even the employment picture doesn't look so bad, certainly compared with the rest of Poland. Naturally, at the outset of the joint venture, there were head-count reductions. But because business was so healthy, the final numbers were not nearly as grim as you might expect. Employment stands at about 3,800, a reduction of 25 percent from when we took over in 1990. There are plenty of companies in Western Europe and the United States that have reduced their head counts by 25 percent and can't show the same performance results.

And Zamech's turnaround goes well beyond numbers. For the first time, the company sold a gas turbine to a major utility in the United States. This was a major victory. There aren't all that many American utilities eager to spend $100 million on Polish equipment. The country still has, as they say, an image problem. So when you see a sale like that, you know the product is absolutely world-class. In fact, this was the first gas turbine of its class ever manufactured in Eastern Europe. That's a huge achievement.

Is the Zamech experience a model for what can happen throughout Eastern Europe?

It's certainly evidence that change is possible. But nothing is guaranteed. We created an island in Poland with Zamech. The company operates more or less independently of everything else going on in the country. That can't last forever. We are exposed to inflation in local supplies. We are exposed to currency fluctuations. We are exposed to changes in the political equation. Over the long term, for Zamech to continue to succeed, Poland, too, must succeed.

It's hard. There are lots of changes in mind-sets, politics, social adjustments. We made three major joint ventures in Poland: Zamech, a company called ABB Dolmel, and a company called Dolmel Drives. Each of the joint ventures was a big success for everyone. Yet in each case, the government minister responsible for the deal paid a political price. The Minister of Privatization I worked with on Zamech resigned under pressure. A government minister I worked with on the two Dolmel companies faced charges that he had done improper things during the negotiations.

There was no substance to any of the charges. Both sides did their work openly, honestly, and ethically. But remember, these were the first three joint ventures in Poland. All three were in the limelight, and not everyone in Poland was in favor of them. It was a big, big change of direction for the country. Not surprisingly, the people who opposed the deals tried to find wrongdoing, and if they couldn't, they just hurled all kinds of charges.

Everyone likes to talk about their success stories. What has been your biggest disappointment?

We've had at least one major disappointment. At the end of 1990, about three months after we began the change program at Zamech, we reached an agreement to buy a turbine factory in the former Yugoslavia. It was a small factory—only about five hundred people worked there—but it was the only turbine factory in the country and it was exceptionally modern for Eastern Europe. It's just outside Zagreb, in what is now Croatia. It was a valuable strategic asset for us.

We did all the things that we did at Zamech. We identified our hungry wolves. We set ambitious performance targets. We taught the mini-MBA, but this time, of course, we translated the cases into Croatian rather than Polish. Then the war with Serbia started. You try to keep making progress, but events that terrible take a toll, both on our ability to help make change and on the performance of the people in the plant.

It was tough for both sides. The people at the Zagreb plant never got the same technical assistance as the people in our other plants; we just couldn't send in as many outside experts from the rest of ABB. In fact, one of my key people from Zurich, a consulting colleague from my days before ABB, was in Zagreb when the war started. All flights out of the country stopped, and we couldn't get him out. So for a full day, working out of Zurich, I did nothing but try to figure how to get this man out of the country. We were monitoring some of the telecommunications traffic, and we learned, quite by accident, that SAS, the Swedish airline, had a plane on the ground. We have a good relationship with SAS. They agreed to wait as we rushed our man from the factory to the airport and got him out. We were lucky.

We weren't so lucky elsewhere. The plant's thirty-year-old director of quality, an important member of our change team, was killed in the fighting. The plant itself was bombed by the Serbians over the Christmas holiday in 1991. The plant manager went to the factory ninety minutes after it was bombed. That gives you a sense of his commitment. The damage wasn't that bad: There were holes in the roof, glass in the machines, nothing we couldn't repair.

The plant manager had to get the news to Zurich, of course, but he was smart enough not to telephone. He figured the Serbs would intercept the calls and send the bombers back. So we communicated by fax. It took about two weeks to get things back to normal. We visited the plant in February, after the fighting had slowed down, to emphasize our commitment to the people there. That plant has yet to make a profit. I hope it will eventually.

That's the hard part of bringing about change.

Bringing about change isn't just hard in Eastern Europe—it's hard anywhere. I got some good training for my work in Eastern Europe when I was consulting for ABB before I signed up for my full-time job. My last big consulting assignment was with the West German subsidiary of ABB. It was our job, working with the top management, to quickly streamline the operations and radically overhaul how the company did business.

We knew the situation was difficult the minute we arrived. There were all kinds of demonstrations. Our early meetings with top management had to be held in a hotel. In fact, as an outside consultant, I was not allowed onto the company's premises. If I tried to enter the headquarters, IG Metall, the big German union, would stage a protest. We had to be extra careful about the security of our papers. In fact, the first thing we did when we got to our hotel was to change the locks on our doors. The atmosphere was very tense, very charged.

It also turned comical at times. I remember working late with my team one night, after we had convinced the union not to protest when we entered the building. It was nine o'clock, we were hungry, so we ordered some pizza. The pizzas were delivered, we ate, and it turned out we had ordered too much, so we gave some pizza to the security guard. We thought we were being nice.

What happens? There is a big story in the next issue of the union newspaper about the terrible consultants at the company. The article made statements like "These consultants don't trust anything here. They won't eat our food; they fly it in from the outside." They made it seem like we were eating caviar rather than pizza we had ordered from down the street. But we got the job done. ABB Germany has been a success. It was a good trial run for what we faced in Poland, Hungary, and elsewhere.

That raises an interesting question. Is the agenda for change in the West really all that different from in the East?

It's not easy to be a European company these days. It's not easy to be a European manager. The process of economic unification, despite the occasional political setbacks, is absolutely going to continue. Unification imposes huge pressures on our companies to improve. We are also under intense pressure from the outside world—the Americans, the Japanese, other players from Asia.

I'm not sure enough people understand the scale of the changes we face. There are some remarkable cost and productivity differentials between countries and companies in Europe. Those differentials are going to have to disappear, and that means lots of difficult adjustments. Today it takes an hour and a half of labor to produce a kilo of butter in Switzerland. It only takes twenty minutes to produce a kilo of butter in Germany and forty minutes in Holland. The butter tastes the same. If you build a house in Switzerland, it takes more than twenty hours of labor for every cubic meter of construction. That same house takes only twelve and a half hours per cubic meter in Germany. Swiss houses aren't that much better than German houses.

How can these productivity differentials go on?

The answer is, they can't. Someone is going to lose. But people are waking up. That's partly because of the boomerang effect of what's happening in Eastern Europe. Think of the impact on companies of what we're doing. Managers and workers in France and Germany and Switzerland realize that there are factories two hours away that can produce exactly the same products with exactly the same quality and 30 percent lower costs. A 30 percent cost disadvantage is a big number. You feel it on the bottom line. You have no choice but to change.

Are you optimistic about the future of Europe?

The process of change will make us stronger. Much of what European companies are learning as they deal with the pressures of the New Europe will help them deal with the challenges of globalization. Or, to put it another way, companies that can't make it in the New Europe certainly aren't going to make it in the rest of the world. It's like a training ground for globalization.

That goes for managers, too. Eastern Europe is a perfect training ground for Western managers. You learn about politics, leadership, change. But more than anything, you learn how to be an entrepreneur: reading your environment, detecting changes, deciding very quickly what to do about them.

The whole world is moving in the direction of

more entrepreneurship. Big companies are decentralizing, breaking down into smaller business units, working as teams, struggling to adjust faster to change. All of that requires managers who think and act like entrepreneurs. And if you want to learn how to be an entrepreneur, how to live by your wits, Eastern Europe is a great place to do it.

CHAPTER 4

THE FINANCIER

JOHN DOERR
Kleiner Perkins Caufield & Byers

The new global economy may be changing the worlds of strategy and management—but it is revolutionizing the world of finance. Money is more mobile and more visible than ever. Just think of the hundreds of billions of dollars in foreign-exchange transactions that take place every day. And yet, precisely because of its mobility, money on its own has become less important than ever. It takes a new kind of financier to make a difference in the New Economy.

Meet John Doerr. At forty-five, Doerr is among America's most accomplished and influential venture capitalists. Most of the companies Doerr funds are headquartered within seventy-five miles of his office in San Francisco, in Silicon Valley, the brutally competitive and compulsively innovative cluster of technology companies from Intel to Apple. Yet the stage on which Doerr plays, and the competitive logic behind what he does, reflect the new realities of doing business around the world.

Not to mention the new realities of business in general. Indeed, Doerr violates almost every stereotype of the cold-blooded venture capitalist—"vulture" capitalist in some entrepreneurial circles. He didn't begin his career in the world of money. Before he got into finance, he was himself a technologist and entrepreneur. He graduated from Rice University with a degree in electrical engineering, holds five patents for computer memory devices, and was the founder of Silicon Compilers, a company that designed software used to design computer chips.

It is this passion for invention and innovation that Doerr has retained in his work in finance. He not only invests in technology companies—Compaq Computer, Sun Microsystems, Lotus Development, Cypress Semiconductor, Intuit, and many others—he also delights in the high-tech products, gadgets, and gizmos that are part of his world. His multilevel home in California, for example, has a computer for each floor; his briefcase is the complete knowledge worker's tool kit, equipped with pager, mobile phone, laptop computer, and more. Practically any new technology product that is launched finds its way to Doerr; he is a one-man beta site. In fact, Doerr's infatuation with the work toys that are part of his profession, and his compulsion for using them at all times, once nearly endangered his life: He was so busy talking on the phone while driving to work one morning that he literally drove off the road. Since then, he has been driven to work each day, allowing him to phone safely.

Despite his prominent role in the cutthroat world of Silicon Valley, Doerr believes that the days of cowboy capitalism are over. The pressures of global competition, the rapid spread of technology, the emergence of new forms of organization, the growing importance of knowledge as the critical competitive resource, have combined to make the stand-alone company a relic. From now on, he argues, business and finance are about forging global alliances and corporate tie-ups that strengthen all sides. Doerr believes that the work of top managers is to create new corporate forms that involve networks and relationships, not only to put together the right capital structure, but also to put together the right knowledge base.

Finally, Doerr doesn't define what he does primarily in terms of making money. Capital isn't what really counts, he says emphatically. What matters is what he brings to start-up ventures: the experience, competitive savvy, and, most important, relationships with companies and allies around the world.

The new global economy, it seems, demands a new kind of global financier. John Doerr fits the profile.

How has globalization changed finance and the way companies compete?

JOHN DOERR: It has made both money and technology less important as factors in corporate success. Today almost all the resources you need to build a successful company are available anywhere in the world. Money and technology are certainly available anywhere, which means, for venture capital, that those two resources don't wield the power they did ten or even five years ago.

Globalization has also reduced the dimensions on which a company can create a sustainable advantage. The half-life of a good idea is much shorter than it used to be. Take Tandem Computers. Tandem was founded in 1974 and went for seven years before it had a real competitor. If your company has a good idea today, you can be sure that within a year a competitor will be financed like a heat-seeking missile to find its way right up your tailpipe. Maybe the company will come from around the corner, maybe it will come from around the world. But it will come.

If money and technology are less important, what has become more important?

Because of globalization, what really matters is the team. The talent you assemble to pursue an opportunity is the only resource your competitors can't duplicate. You've heard the cliché that the three factors for success in real estate are location, location, location. In venture capital, the three critical success factors are team, team, team.

That's an interesting twist: Globalization makes people more important than ever. Can you say more about why?

Global competition has changed the entire fabric of the economy. We no longer live and work in the old-style capitalist economy, where competitive advantage is based on labor or natural resources. We live in an economy driven by the knowledge that we create. That new reality changes how you look at every aspect of doing business, how you make sense of the competitive environment.

When I look at a map of the world, for example, I don't visualize it in terms of miles or even countries. Instead I see Internet packages or E-mail messages flowing between various points. If you drew the kind of map that I'm talking about, you'd find that Boston, Massachusetts, is adjacent to Palo Alto, California—the amount of electronic traffic between those two points is just incredible. You'd also find an incredible amount of traffic from Seattle down the West Coast, from San Diego through south San Francisco, among all the life sciences companies that are competing and collaborating with one another.

In this new economy, venture capital is about investing in the entrepreneurs who are sending those messages, exchanging those ideas. The reason is simple: If you live in a knowledge economy, you invest in the people who are creating and sharing knowledge. If you are not "on the net," you're really out of it.

Are these changes happening only for high-technology companies, or are they happening across the board?

Any industry anywhere in the world is susceptible to reinvention by a group of people who bring new knowledge to that industry. With innovation, creativity, technology, and a sprinkling of capital, you can transform everything from shoes to steel to home entertainment. It's happened! Just look at Nike and Nucor and Nintendo. The role of the venture capitalist in this new economy is to work with a company's management team to focus on what knowledge the company can deliver to add value precisely where the market needs it. The closer you come to making the connection between your added value and the market's need, the greater the rewards.

Give us a more detailed description of the role of the venture capitalist. Where do you fit in the new global economy?

Venture capitalists don't belong on center stage. Our role is very much a supporting one. But even

though we play a supporting role, it is often critical. We pull back the curtains, run the lights, and
do all the work required to support the performers
onstage, the entrepreneurs. And that's where the
problem is today, particularly if your goal is to create a company with high production values. There
are plenty of good ideas, plenty of great entrepreneurs. Our problem isn't the budget deficit or the
trade deficit: It's a management deficit, a team
deficit. And incidentally, there is a shortage of true
value-added venture capitalists, those who know
how to run the lights and curtains, who have been
through the up-and-down cycle, who can really
help a team maneuver through hard times.

*Why is it so important for a venture capitalist to
have gone through the up-and-down cycle in an
industry?*

In the 1980s we saw a group of companies rein-
vent the computing industry. These were new companies, with zero revenues at the start of the
decade and revenues of $100 billion at the end of
the decade. The combined market value of those
companies was more than $100 billion. It was the
single largest new creation of wealth in the history
of the planet.

Today we're looking at a totally different competitive map. The rules of competition have
changed again. Some of the entrepreneurs are the
same, but most of them are different. More important, the market logic is different. With so much

change, the role of the venture capitalist becomes critical.

But let's be clear: I'm not talking about money. Smart entrepreneurs know where they can get capital. They know there's more venture money under the roof of one building on Sand Hill Road in Silicon Valley than there is in the entire state of Texas or entire countries in Europe. Money is neither a mystery nor a constraint.

The critical element is experience. It's a certain kind of business knowledge, the ability to evaluate business models, to help build teams, to help teams execute. Real knowledge comes from living through a down cycle and seeing who wins and who loses.

You say that venture capitalists play a supporting role. What does that mean on a day-to-day basis?

My job really boils down to four tasks, from seven in the morning until nine at night. First, we help build teams, evaluate managers, recruit new talent, and help teams work better. Second, we raise money and assemble resources. Third, we build teams. And fourth, we raise more money. That's what we do, day in, day out: build teams and assemble resources.

Our role is to be an honest broker and to use our relationships with these players to put together the strongest team possible. That's what venture capitalists should do. We don't run the companies that we invest in, and money isn't the most important asset we contribute. The most important asset is the scar tissue that we have to show for past efforts. In the global economy, where business leaders face totally new challenges, that's how we add value.

How would you describe the new challenges business leaders face?

In the past, entrepreneurs started businesses. Today entrepreneurs invent new business models. That's a big difference, and it comes back to global competition. One important impact of globalization is that businesspeople in the United States, for example, are suddenly confronted with entirely different business models from other parts of the world. The way the Japanese structure a company, the way they build relationships among companies, or the way they define the fundamental value proposition behind a product is different from what American executives are used to. Likewise, the Europeans are different in their own ways.

These differences, and the competitive pressures they unleash, have stimulated American entrepreneurs to create many new and untraditional business models. Today the critical measure of the genius of any venture is not the market that it's in, but the way it's in that market—the business model it uses to beat the competition.

If competition is about contending business models, how does that change the role of the financier?

What's pivotal is the knowledge of the industry the venture capitalist brings. It's the analytical framework he or she applies to the business opportunity.

I like to say we earn the right to advise entrepreneurs. What counts is the power of your insights, the experiences you've garnered, and the mistakes that you've made, ideally building a company of your own. When you sit down to advise entrepreneurs on how to build their businesses, it helps enormously if you've been a successful entrepreneur yourself. Venture capitalists who really add value have earned a master's degree from the school of hard knocks in engineering business models. You can't win arguments with voting control. The best idea must win.

How do you evaluate the merits of different business models?

You must evaluate business models on a relative basis: How do they stack up against the competition? And you must evaluate them over time: Does the model evolve as the business evolves? A winning business model will deliver a compelling advantage to a large, unserved, or poorly served market. It's also extremely desirable if the model is so radical and so pointed that the competition can't respond to it without essentially receiving a javelin. Entrenched competitors shouldn't be able to adopt your model without doing economic, social, even spiritual violence to the way they think about their businesses. They should have to turn themselves inside out. That's the mark of a great competitive business model.

Can you give us an example of how a company used a new business model to mount a successful competitive challenge?

Think about the way Compaq took apart IBM in the personal-computer business using the IBM-established channel of distribution. Or how the clone makers at Dell subsequently, if only temporarily, assaulted Compaq's position. It's not that the managers at any of those companies were asleep; they weren't dumb or bad or incompetent. They just had a business model that was working for them and making lots of money—for a while. As a consequence, their over-the-horizon radar for changes in their business model was shut off when a new model came along.

Compaq used some very different ideas about how to compete to rise to prominence at IBM's expense. But they had no idea what it would mean to go head-to-head with the business model developed by Michael Dell. He was able to sell computers at half the profit margin, half the investment in R&D, and with one-fourth the investment in marketing and sales. That's a power-fully different model, which provoked radical change at Compaq.

You've described how the world of companies and competition has changed. What about changes in the world of finance itself?

Twenty years ago venture capital was a rich man's club. A group of wealthy individuals would meet for lunch periodically at the Palo Alto Club. Each one would introduce his projects to the others to see if they could come up with the $150,000 it took to launch a new venture. Every offering was syndicated, and no one invested more than $25,000 in any one project.

That was the 1970s. By the early 1980s, the business had changed. It had evolved into professional partnerships. Instead of meeting for lunch at the club, venture capitalists would search for entrepreneurs from a garage—Apple Computer—or from a House of Pancakes—Compaq. Instead of raising $150,000, we raised $1.5 million to develop the first product, take it to market, and see if it worked.

That second era of venture capital is just as irrelevant today as the first era was in the 1980s. Today, large global companies are much more aggressive, much more alert to new market opportunities, much more driven to grow new businesses. Whether it's AT&T or Matsushita or Bell Atlantic or TCI, big global companies are thoughtfully exploring joint ventures, strategic alliances with start-ups. I call these co-ventures. As a consequence, venture capitalists today are in the business of creating new working relationships.

Is that as true in other countries as it is in the United States? What about Japan, for example?

Venture capital in Japan is dramatically different from venture capital in the United States. There's a lot more lending and a lot less risk-taking. In Japan it is illegal for a venture capitalist to serve on the board of a company. But building relationships is still a critical element. In fact, one of the critical roles we play for Kleiner Perkins companies is to help build relationships in Japan that allow them to compete and win—big time.

For example, we've worked closely with two partners in Tokyo, TechnoVenture and Nippon Enterprise Developers. We worked with them to create a phenomenally successful Japanese operation for Sun Microsystems—to the point where Sun's share of the workstation market in Japan is double what it is worldwide. A big factor behind Sun's success was its ability to persuade a major figure from the Japanese computer industry, a man named Dr. Kohei Amo, to leave the Toshiba board and run Sun's operation in Japan.

It was a major coup, and it was all about relationships. Dr. Yaichi Ayukawa, the founder of TechnoVenture and the son of the founder of the Nissan keiretsu, was a grade-school classmate of another man, named Mr. [Hiroaki] Ueda, who ran the Nippon Enterprise Development Corporation. The two of them went to visit Amo on behalf of Sun. Not only was Amo a graduate of Stanford, which meant he already knew about Sun, and not only was he a member of the board of Toshiba, which meant he was a top computer-industry figure in Japan, but he was also a grade-school classmate of both Ayukawa and Ueda. Eventually they convinced Amo to become general manager of upstart Sun.

That decision was a key break in Sun's effort to build a locally managed subsidiary that really kicked butt in Japan. We played a big role, but the issue wasn't money. It was assembling the right resources: people and credibility.

You keep emphasizing that money isn't the venture capitalist's main asset. On the other hand, hasn't globalization made it more expensive to compete?

Over the past decade the amount of money it takes to create a great company has gone up substantially. The stakes are much higher. Competitors are more nimble, they can come from anywhere in the world, and the big companies are no longer asleep.

Genentech is the pioneer company in recombinant DNA biotechnology. Back in 1972 it was founded with $10,000 per month in funding for R&D. Kleiner Perkins was the single largest investor. Our total investment was only $120,000. In computing it took only $1.5 million for Compaq to get to market with its first portable computer. Compaq sold $110 million worth of PCs the following year. Those kinds of numbers look ridiculously small today. The ante has certainly increased.

What hasn't changed is the importance of getting the real risk out of the way up front. The best way to make a lot of money in a new venture, to create lots of value for you, your team, and your shareholders, is to be ruthlessly honest about the real risks in the business. Eliminate those risks with the first round of money you raise. If you take the first $1 million that goes into your project and use it to remove all the real business risk in an attractive venture, I guarantee we can raise all the additional capital needed at favorable terms.

That sounds great, but how do you think about eliminating risk from a new business early on?

Caesar divided all of Gaul into three parts. I divide all risk into four parts. First is technical risk. To me that's a wonderful risk. That's a risk we like to take on and remove with finite early dollars. In a phrase, can you split the atom? Splice the gene? Crack the code? The second risk is what we hate the most: market risk. It's the trickiest part of the whole recipe. Will the dog eat the dog food? Will the fish jump out of the tank?

The third type of risk is people risk. The dirty

little secret in Silicon Valley is that most CEOs are replaced. In fact, it happens in roughly two-thirds of the ventures we back. And even if the CEO makes it, I've never seen a venture where all the co-founders are still together four years into the project. Most teams simply don't stay together.

The fourth and final risk is financing risk. That's the easiest risk to deal with. No worthwhile venture should fail because it ran out of money. If it's a good project, we ought to be able to get the capital to fund it. I'd say your venture backer has two responsibilities above all others: to make sure a good team is in place, and to make sure the project doesn't run out of money.

We've talked a lot about competition in general. How about the world of the entrepreneur in particular? Has it experienced big changes as a result of globalization?

I hope this overstatement emphasizes the point: It's no longer possible for an independent high-tech start-up to succeed. Today, when we make a decision about whether to invest in a new company, one of the most important questions we ask is, Who will be your corporate partners? What big companies can bring special resources to this business, accelerate its growth, and reduce its risk?

The conventional wisdom about Silicon Valley is that it's filled with wild-eyed and woolly entrepreneurs who are totally independent, who absolutely insist on succeeding or failing on their own merits—you know, cowboy capitalism and the Wild West. That may have been true in the past. It's definitely not true today.

I see something completely different: The overarching objective in this new global economy is to assemble an array of partners around the world, a network of allies, that allows you to win against global rivals. As venture capitalists, we're looking for corporate partners who will commit to a project and raise their own risk profile. I don't mean corporate equivocators, hedging their bets. In other words, the project is so important to them, they're willing to increase the risk to their own business by participating.

It sounds as if venture capitalists have to be much more aggressive than in the past.

This is no longer a business of responding to business plans that get mailed to us or tossed over the transom. We're not waiting for people to come to us with their ideas—although when they do, we read their plans and pay attention.

Today we identify our own targets and clearly establish priorities. We highly prize a few key ideas we think are really going to matter. We analyze broad themes in the economy. We look at how technology is evolving, how it will affect people's lives, what's technologically possible, what will make a difference. From that analysis we develop initiatives.

What do you mean by an initiative?

An initiative is a commitment by my partnership to focus our resources on one particular area. It's not just a lucky single investment by an individual partner in a company. Instead it's a commitment by all my partners to catalyze, help fund an industry.

We start by writing a meta-plan for an industry. Then we tear it to shreds, the same way we would any other plan that comes into our shop. We'll meet off-site for days to decide whether it measures up, and whether we should make it an initiative. Once we do, every partner pitches in. We budget the amount of money we want to invest in it. We network aggressively to become expert in that field. Then finally, we incubate specific companies and lead investments.

Initiatives are another major change from the way venture capital used to work. In the 1980s specialization was a key way for venture capitalists to compete and add value. Firms organized themselves as life sciences groups, information sciences groups, and communications groups. Today specialization is necessary but not sufficient. You have to specialize and anticipate, identify and incubate great opportunities.

What's an example of an initiative?

One example we see coming over the horizon is in the field of the life sciences, in particular the area of genomics. We think the human genome project is going to succeed in about half the time that was originally projected. In other words, in the next five years we will have identified all 100,000 human genes. We'll know where they are. We already know that there are roughly 1,300 serious human diseases, from breast cancer to colon cancer, that are genetic in origin. In the near future we're going to know where on the three billion base pairs of genes the genetic defect is that is associated with a particular disease.

That's going to change the whole paradigm of drug discovery. It will change the whole practice of health care. We are right now decoding the most interesting software program that's ever been written—the human genetic sequence. I think it's a technological change that is as important as the computer chip. That qualifies as an initiative for us, one that we're already investing in.

With all the opportunities you have to make investments, what specific factors determine which companies you invest in?

A key question we've tried to answer is, What makes for a truly great company? When you look at the $100 billion in market value created by the computing industry, the overwhelming majority of it comes from about twelve companies. Literally hundreds of companies have been swept away in the creation of that $100 billion in value. We've analyzed 170 companies that we invested in, trying to isolate the attributes that make up a truly winning company, the characteristics that separate the big winners not only from the big losers but from the so-so companies.

Five attributes distinguish truly great companies. I think they're required for any company anywhere in the world to achieve greatness. At the time that we invested in the companies that became huge successes, none possessed all five. But whether they're in computers or life sciences, bits and bytes, or bugs and drugs, great companies quickly develop these five characteristics: a commitment to technical excellence, experienced management, a strategic focus on a large or rapidly growing market, reasonable financings, and a sense of urgency.

Let's run through them one at a time.

First, a commitment to technical excellence. I don't mean published papers or the number of Ph.D.'s on the payroll. I mean a commitment on the part of the founders to win in the worldwide scramble for talent. You must create and maintain a culture of technical excellence within the company.

It's essential that you start with the right people and the right culture. If the people you want on your team think they can contribute and make a difference—if they can learn, advance their careers, develop their own personal, professional, and corporate-knowledge assets—then they'll sign up. Those opportunities matter more than stock options, bonuses, or 401(k) plans. That's why the best people want to work for companies like Silicon Graphics and Sun Microsystems instead of Garagetronics. It's particularly true in Silicon Valley, where you can change your job without changing where you park your car. The pressure must be on for technical excellence from the very beginning.

What's an example of the importance of technical excellence?

Take Sun Microsystems. One of my current partners, Vinod Khosla, was founding CEO of Sun. Before Sun he was a cofounder of Daisy, a leading workstation company in the early days. However, one day the Daisy board of cofounders summarily tossed him out of the company. So Vinod simply changed directions slightly—instead of making a dedicated workstation like Daisy made, he concluded that there ought to be a large market for a general-purpose workstation. Large enough even to change the direction of computing.

He got his buddy Scott McNealy—who had worked in an FMC military tank factory in San Jose and screwed together computers on an assembly line at Onyx, a now-defunct microcomputer manufacturer—to join him in this new company.

They both knew, without ever having to say it, that to win they would need technical excellence.

At that time I was a very young venture capitalist hanging around Stanford. Vinod and I knew an amazing German computer designer, a guy named Andy Bechtolsheim, who was designing the equivalent of Porsche computers—the highest-performance computers in the world—but using VW parts. There was absolutely no doubt that we wanted Andy to build the computer that would take down Digital Equipment Company.

That wasn't enough. We also knew we needed the same kind of technical excellence in software. But we didn't know who the Andy Bechtolsheim of software was. So we began interviewing, going through résumés, working the network, asking friends of friends who was the best. A candidate would interview with Vinod and Scott and in their judgment wouldn't be quite great enough. But they ended every interview by asking, "If you got this job, who would you like to see on your team with you?"

Finally, after months of interviewing, they hit on the name of another genius, Bill Joy. At the time Bill was in Berkeley, where, on a not-for-profit basis, he was replacing the operating system that came free on DEC's VAX minicomputers with his version of AT&T's Unix. Bill did that for almost one-third of DEC's installed base—a remarkable feat.

I'll never forget Andy Bechtolsheim's reaction when Vinod told him that all the interviews had led to the conclusion that Bill Joy should lead the software effort. Andy said, "I know Bill Joy. That's a great idea. Why didn't we go after him in the first place?" At that point Vinod nearly strangled Andy.

But instead, that afternoon Khosla, McNealy, and Bechtolsheim piled into Andy's small VW sedan, drove up to Berkeley, and persuaded Bill Joy to abandon his doctoral thesis and cofound Sun Microsystems. Bill Joy soon recruited a half-dozen world-class programmers from MIT, Carnegie-Mellon, and Xerox PARC. Suddenly Sun became the place to be, the place where the very best work was being done. They assembled a team in the information sciences that was the business equivalent of the all-time all-star baseball team.

And remember, the initial capitalization of Sun was $1.5 million. Sun was profitable every year thereafter. The venture-capital dollars were a tiny pilot light. What really mattered was the early commitment to technical excellence.

What's the second critical factor for a great company?

The second factor is experienced management. To stay with Sun Microsystems: It's true that Vinod Khosla had never been a CEO before and Scott McNealy had never been more than a director of manufacturing. In fact, the founding team of

Sun consisted of four twenty-seven-year-old kids backed by a pretty naive thirty-year-old venture capitalist. In part we were successful because we didn't know it couldn't be done.

But we also had the good sense to add people to the team who had more than done the job before. So we hired as our vice-president of engineering Bernie Lacroute, who had been, in effect, the chief technical officer at DEC. Bernie's nickname at DEC was Little Napoleon. He was very tough, smart, disciplined, and driven. Bernie joined Sun when it was a dinky little $4-million-per-year engineering workstation company. When he left, it was a $2-billion-per-year distributed computing company. Sun's founders drew heavily on Bernie's experience, and that of many others, to make it happen.

But don't large and often declining companies also have experienced management? Why doesn't experience translate into success?

There's a different kind of experienced management that's necessary to create a great company. The reason so many large companies are in trouble today—and not just in the United States—is that "experienced" management has come to mean people who are interested in maintaining their current income, protecting their perks or their bonuses, or pursuing some abstract theory of what makes good managers.

Great companies are made by managers who are married to their enterprise. Managers who act like, think like, and are owners of the business. People who are risk-takers, who are passionate about the business in a way that goes beyond the job. People for whom it's not just a paycheck, it's not strictly business. It's very personal.

What's the third attribute of a great company?

The third factor is strategic focus on a large or rapidly growing market. The best example of this is Lotus. In its early years, Mitch Kapor, its founder, had an incredible sense of the kind of performance excellence that would define the IBM personal computer. In fact, I contend that in the beginning, IBM's machine wasn't really a PC—it was a machine designed to run Lotus 1-2-3.

Lotus started with a strategic focus on the market's strike zone, the large and rapidly growing part of the personal-computing industry. For a half-dozen years it was more than a small burr under Bill Gates's saddle that Lotus was a larger and more successful software company than Microsoft. And Lotus did it with strategic focus. However, the focus fuzzed, Mitch left, and Lotus lost its momentum. Jeff Raikes, Microsoft's senior VP of U.S. sales and marketing, focused so intensely, so personally, on competing with Lotus and WordPerfect that he knew the names and ages of his rivals' children.

What's the fourth factor?

The fourth is reasonable financings—with the emphasis on *reasonable*. I've seen companies raise too much money as well as too little, and you can raise it at the wrong time.

As an example, consider Caremark. At the time we made our investment it was called Home Health Care of America. They believed that they could take seriously but not fatally ill patients— people who were going to be fed through holes in their chest cavities, often for the rest of their lives—out of hospitals and deliver that service in the home. It would mean an improvement in the patients' quality of life, a lowering of the cost of care, and it would address a problem that was an important part of the nation's overall health-care concern.

The entrepreneurs came to us and said, "Let's roll this thing out nationally. It will take $2.5 million to do it." We feared that $2.5 million was too much money, too soon. Instead, less than thirty days after our first meeting, we wrote a check for $600,000. It was enough money to prove with a test whether we could make the business work in Cleveland, Ohio. If it worked in Cleveland, then we could scale it up to the rest of the country.

Three things happened because we wrote them a check for $600,000 instead of $2.5 million. First, we only risked $600,000. Second, the entrepreneurs owned a much larger percentage of their company. And third, when the test worked and we did raise the next round of capital, the price was four times higher than it had been eight months earlier. Today that company is worth $4 billion.

And the fifth factor?

The fifth and final factor that defines a great company is a sense of urgency. This is something we all understand; you've felt it when you walk in to visit an organization that's really on the move.

Urgency is the ally of a new venture. It's the advantage a more nimble organization has over larger companies with slow-moving bureaucracies, entrenched marketing operations, installed bases, and paralyzed decision-making processes. A company with one great new idea, a smaller budget, and a fleet-of-foot team has all the advantages.

As you think about the larger role you play as a venture capitalist, how do you define success?

Part of my job is to make the shares of stock in the companies we fund as valuable as possible. At the same time, I want to be a part of a team that creates enterprises that are going to be durable, permanent players in the global economy. I'm very proud of the fact that eight of the companies we helped finance from the beginning are now in the Fortune 500. That's a sign of staying power.

But what really excites me is seeing teams come together with new technology to make products and services that change and improve the way people live. Let me give you an example. One of my partners, Brook Byers, incubated a company called Hybritech that created something called PSAB. It's a test that identifies prostate cancer early enough so the disease can be treated successfully. Brook dreamed up this company on the back of a napkin at an airport in 1976 and went on to be the founding CEO.

Hybritech was bought by Lily and now it's worth $1.5 billion. But who really cares what it's worth? My estimate is that the company has saved fifteen thousand lives. That wouldn't have happened if the company hadn't been started. When Hybritech saves you or your father from prostate cancer, that's a really deep kind of success.

Which is more important to you—making a difference or making a profit?

Most of what we do is designed to combine those two in a meaningful way. If you look at the reinvention of the computer industry, the breakthroughs in genetics, they both make a difference and make a profit. But if you forced me to choose, I'd vote for making a difference. My partners would, too. When I look at the projects that we decide to get involved in, we're not interested in a quick flip, where we get out of the project as soon as we can after the initial public offering. We're interested in how durable the enterprise is. When we make our investment decisions, we're not just guided by the tyranny of internal rate of return or market values. We're guided by the values we share. Those values put making a difference first, and making a profit second.

FOR THE BEST IN PAPERBACKS, LOOK FOR THE

In every corner of the world, on every subject under the sun, Penguin represents quality and variety—the very best in publishing today.

For complete information about books available from Penguin—including Puffins, Penguin Classics, and Arkana—and how to order them, write to us at the appropriate address below. Please note that for copyright reasons the selection of books varies from country to country.

In the United Kingdom: Please write to *Dept. JC, Penguin Books Ltd, FREEPOST, West Drayton, Middlesex UB7 0BR.*

If you have any difficulty in obtaining a title, please send your order with the correct money, plus ten percent for postage and packaging, to *P.O. Box No. 11, West Drayton, Middlesex UB7 0BR*

In the United States: Please write to *Consumer Sales, Penguin USA, P.O. Box 999, Dept. 17109, Bergenfield, New Jersey 07621-0120.* VISA and MasterCard holders call 1-800-253-6476 to order all Penguin titles

In Canada: Please write to *Penguin Books Canada Ltd, 10 Alcorn Avenue, Suite 300, Toronto, Ontario M4V 3B2*

In Australia: Please write to *Penguin Books Australia Ltd, P.O. Box 257, Ringwood, Victoria 3134*

In New Zealand: Please write to *Penguin Books (NZ) Ltd, Private Bag 102902, North Shore Mail Centre, Auckland 10*

In India: Please write to *Penguin Books India Pvt Ltd, 706 Eros Apartments, 56 Nehru Place, New Delhi 110 019*

In the Netherlands: Please write to *Penguin Books Netherlands bv, Postbus 3507, NL-1001 AH Amsterdam*

In Germany: Please write to *Penguin Books Deutschland GmbH, Metzlerstrasse 26, 60594 Frankfurt am Main*

In Spain: Please write to *Penguin Books S. A., Bravo Murillo 19, 1° B, 28015 Madrid*

In Italy: Please write to *Penguin Italia s.r.l., Via Felice Casati 20, I-20124 Milano*

In France: Please write to *Penguin France S. A., 17 rue Lejeune, F-31000 Toulouse*

In Japan: Please write to *Penguin Books Japan, Ishikiribashi Building, 2-5-4, Suido, Bunkyo-ku, Tokyo 112*

In Greece: Please write to *Penguin Hellas Ltd, Dimocritou 3, GR-106 71 Athens*

In South Africa: Please write to *Longman Penguin Southern Africa (Pty) Ltd, Private Bag X08, Bertsham 2013*